Gender, Madness, Theology

UNTIL
AT
DAWN
WE
WAKE

Charlotte Dalwood

Unless otherwise noted, [Scripture quotations are from] New Revised Standard Version Bible, copyright © 1989 National Council of the Churches of Christ in the United States of America. Used by permission. All rights reserved worldwide.

THE HOLY BIBLE, NEW INTERNATIONAL VERSION®, NIV® Copyright © 1973, 1978, 1984, 2011 by Biblica, Inc.® Used by permission. All rights reserved worldwide.

Copyright © 2024 by Charlotte Dalwood
First Edition

Cover Design by Matthew J. Distefano
Cover Image by Keith Giles
Interior Layout by Matthew J. Distefano

Print ISBN 978-1-964252-24-7
Electronic ISBN 978-1-964252-28-5
Printed in the United States of America

Published by Quoir
Chico, California
www.quoir.com

CONTENTS

ACKNOWLEDGEMENTS VII

PART ONE 1

1. I, Ezekiel 3

2. DSM Dreams 11

3. The Paths Ahead 19

PART TWO 23

4. Madness, Neurodivergence 25

5. Disability and the Seventh Day 37

PART THREE 51

6. The Valley of the Shadow of Death 53

7. The Serpent's Bite 69

PART FOUR 89

8. Paranoid Reading, Paranoia 93

9. Being Damned, Being Trans 103

PART FIVE 123

10. A Future for Eve 127

11. A Past for Adam   139

PART SIX   153

12. Until At Dawn We Wake   157

Endnotes   167

For Steph and Travis
who saw it firsthand
—and—
For Ellery
the brightest star in my night sky

ACKNOWLEDGEMENTS

THIS IS A BOOK about the social. It is fitting, therefore, that it was written with the support of a community of readers, friends, and family. Many thanks to everyone who read and commented on earlier versions of this book and encouraged me to keep going.

As iron sharpens iron, my teachers at Ambrose University, Yale University, and the University of Calgary have honed my writing and critical thinking skills over the years. Their influence is apparent in everything that follows.

Some of the essays that follow first appeared, in part, in an earlier form in other publications: *Earth & Altar*, *rabble.ca*, *Religion Dispatches*, *The Episcopal Café*, *Theology & Sexuality*, and *Xtra Magazine*. I am grateful to the editors of those publications for first giving my writing voice a home.

Thank you to Keith and Matthew at Quoir for seeing the promise in a little book like this and taking a chance.

Rabbi Mark Glickman and I had many fruitful conversations about disability, life, and faith as I wrote this book. Thank you for helping me focus my ideas and for encouraging me to write this loving farewell letter to the Christians who raised me.

Special thanks to the community at Temple B'nai Tikvah for welcoming me home.

To the doctors, nurses, and therapists who have walked with me as I ventured through the realm of the unreal—especially my psychiatrists Dr. Addington and Dr. Cassity; my case manager and nurse, Sogna; and my psychologist, Amy: thank you, from the bottom of my heart.

Therese and Jim took me under their wing and helped me to stand strong when the psychosis came back and threatened to knock me down: thank you.

It is no exaggeration to say I would not be here were it not for my two best friends, Steph and Travis (to whom this book is dedicated in part). You two kept me alive: words cannot express how grateful I am for all you have done, but maybe I can buy you a beer sometime?

My lovely fiancé, Ellery, fell in love with all of me, including the schizophrenic parts. You're the reason I get up each morning, El. I love you lots and lots and lots.

PART ONE
Intersections

"Thou art a scholar; speak to it, Horatio."

Hamlet, Act 1, Scene 1

One

I, EZEKIEL

AT MY SICKEST, I believed myself to be the reincarnation of the Hebrew prophet Ezekiel.

I spent hours poring over the prophet's eponymous Old Testament text.[1] Every word, every verse contained a message just for me.

I was a prophet. Chosen by God to carry a message of doom to the people. But first I had to prove myself and receive my prophetic word.

"Then God said to me, 'Son of man, eat this scroll I am giving you and fill your stomach with it.' So I ate it, and it tasted as sweet as honey in my mouth" (Ezekiel 3:3, NIV).

Just as God commanded, I tore pages out of my Bible and consumed them. And they filled me with a warmth I've only ever felt during the clearest moments of connection with the Divine.

Ezekiel the Schizophrenic?

More than any other Old Testament prophet, Ezekiel's eccentric—at times bizarre—visions and behaviours have inspired posthumous speculation about his psychological state.

Catalepsy, seizures, hysteria—all of these and more have been proposed as after-the-fact diagnoses.[2] But the one that resonates most closely with me is the diagnostic sign under which I travel: schizophrenia.

"Like the writings of schizophreniacs [*sic*]," wrote Edwin Broome, Jr., in an influential mid-twentieth century article for the *Journal of Biblical*

Literature, "the writings of Ezekiel are difficult to follow: rules of ordinary logic simply do not apply."[3] Stretches of catatonic "freezing" (Ezekiel 4:4-8); paranoid worries about being rejected by the people of Israel (e.g., Ezekiel 2:5-7); and, of course, the supernatural voices that he hears—all indicate that Ezekiel was on the schizophrenia spectrum, or so scholars like Broome would have us believe.

And maybe they're right. But if so, so what?

Does it matter one way or the other if Ezekiel was mad? Does it matter if I am?

Discerning the Voice of God

I have heard the voice of God, clear as a summer day, commanding me to prophesy.

I have heard the voice of God, warm as a summer breeze, calling me to a life of reflection on God's Word.

One of these is the result of dopamine imbalances in my brain. The other is the reason I went to seminary.

Only one of these is "real." Only one of these "counts."

———

Christians are very good at subjecting the abnormal to discernment.

Women's ordination, the inclusion of 2SLGBTQ+ people in the life of the Church, switching from in-person to digital worship—all of these require intense and protracted prayer and debate. Because they're unusual, or, at least, because they seem to be.

The commonplace passes without reflection. Most Christians don't think about the flag at the altar rail (in the United States, at least); it has always been there. Of course God called that cisgender,[4] heterosexual white man to ordained ministry; we can trust that God speaks to that kind of body.

And there's something idolatrous about Christians' uncritical acceptance of the ordinary.

It's not that the ordinary is necessarily bad. It's that, as theologian Paul Tillich defined idolatry nearly a century ago, "something essentially conditioned is taken as unconditional, something essentially partial is boosted into universality, and something essentially finite is given infinite significance."[5]

Christians divinize the ordinary and demonize the extraordinary by uncritically assuming that God is present in what they know and absent in what they don't.

And, so, Christians accept that the person who feels a burning desire to undertake ordained ministry is hearing the voice of God. That's how God speaks.

Whereas "obviously" the person who audibly hears the Divine voice cannot be trusted. God doesn't speak to "us" that way. There's nothing Christians can learn from "them."

After all, they're mad.

It is ableist indeed to exclude schizophrenics from the ambit of God's revelatory activities in the world.[6] Too, it betrays a rather low view of God's ability to make Godself known in and through the disabling experiences of this life.

That said, there *is* something qualitatively different about a schizophrenic episode and an instance of Divine self-disclosure, something that the former only simulates.

In the Christian Scriptures, the Word of God is terrifying, incisive, and sometimes rejected—but it is never unclear. When God speaks, you know it is God speaking.

That's what distinguishes the Voice of God from the voice my illness told me was of God.

In psychosis, you lose the ability to distinguish what is of the world from what is of your mind. Everything is real—the hallucinations and delusions all.

There's the key difference. The Word of God is not real. Not because it is "false" or "non-existent." But because it is not of this world, a thing among other things, like a stapler or a song. Nor is it of the mind, an idea among others, like theology or dinner plans. It exists in both but is not reducible to either.

And when you hear the Word, in whatever form it might take, that fact is clear.

The Word of God precedes and exceeds creation; it comes before, and it extends beyond. And when it enters into the created world, it rends reality apart: precisely because it is not a part *of* creation, it is what *creates*. Hence the frequent New Testament refrain of the heavens opening—that is to say, of reality tearing (in the Greek: *schizo*, the root of schizophrenia)—during visions of the eternal (see, e.g., Mark 1:10).

When God speaks, this world is shown to be partial. There is something else "out there" in the space beyond what we can normally see, hear, and touch. And knowledge of that fact overwhelms.

Perhaps that is why, when the angel first appeared to the Virgin Mary, it was with the words "Do not be afraid" (Luke 1:30). Fear is the natural response to revelation. And wonder.

The Schizophrenic Sublime

If God speaks to schizophrenics—as I am convinced God speaks to all God's people—it is in spite of our schizophrenia. Much as God always speaks to people in spite of our creaturely limitations, whatever those may be. But there is nevertheless something about the experience of psychosis that offers unique insight into the ways God speaks to dis/abled bodies, something those who have never shared in that experience can only come to understand through the testimony of those of us who have.

This is not to romanticize psychosis. There is nothing romantic about a schizophrenic episode. It is a terrifying, disorienting ordeal.

But there *is* something sublime: an experience of beauty born of dread.

When you travel beyond the borders of reality and return again, what you're left with is awe.

Awe at the fragility of the real. Awe at the vistas that resolve into view when reality shatters.

I experience schizophrenia as the re-enchantment of the world. Angels and demons are everywhere, spiritual forces are at work in the smallest of happenings, God speaks to me as clearly as he did to the Old Testament prophets.

It is a frightening world to inhabit. But it is also beautiful in its marvels.

In psychosis, the mind simulates the inbreaking of another reality into this one that occurs in actuality during moments of Divine self-disclosure. Reality is shown to be "more than" what one previously thought. The veil between the real and the unreal is pierced, and things we can only imagine are revealed to us.

Those things aren't "real," of course. But that doesn't mean the experience of encountering them has nothing to teach us.

Indeed, the schizophrenic sublime is such that those who have experienced psychosis know more fully—if still only approximately—what it is like to hear the Word of God than those who have not. Simply because we schizophrenics who have ventured to reality's edge and returned again are experienced enough to know not to idolize the real.

We know better than to equate the empirical with the universal; to take what we can see, hear, and feel one day as the extent of what is. Our horizons are forever haunted by the advent of something more: another hallucination, another delusion, another reason to be paranoid.

Because reality is frail. Its bounds are porous. And if it is permeable, that is because reality isn't all there is. There's something else beyond.

I would call that something "God."

Which is why Ezekiel the "mad" prophet is a prophet nonetheless. Even we schizophrenics have much to teach Christians.

This Is My Body, This My Schizophrenic Mind

Ezekiel's consumption of the scroll is Eucharistic.

The scroll contained "words of lament and mourning and woe" (Ezekiel 2:10). But in a more substantial sense the scroll contained the Word, that which empowered Ezekiel to give voice to the prophetic revelations of God.

Depth psychology—exemplified by the work of Sigmund Freud—understands schizophrenia to be the inbreaking of the mind's reality into the external world. Where schizophrenia breaks the boundary separating inner from outer reality, Divine revelation breaks the boundary between the Creator and creation. Different breaks, but breaks all the same.

For liturgically minded Christians, the latter one comes into focus most clearly in the Eucharist. Bread and wine become the body and blood of the Word incarnate. Through Christians' consumption of these elements, they are united with the perfect revelation of God in Jesus Christ. "Assumed by Christ," theologian Kathryn Tanner explains in *Jesus, Humanity, and the Trinity*, "Christ becomes the subject of our acts in much the way the second Person of the Trinity is the subject of Jesus' acts. Our acts are Christ's acts, we can say Christ acts when we act, in so far as what we are and do comes by way of the power of Christ."[7] Creature and Creator come together in a non-competitive correspondence of action that empowers the former to act beyond our limitations as fallen creation.

Transcendence and immanence intersect for humanity's benefit.

———

When reality breaks, anything is possible. Angels can whisper divine secrets in our ears. The devil can walk in our midst. Something as simple as the play of shadows on the sidewalk can contain abiding personal significance.

It is the contingency of reality that we schizophrenics know firsthand. Nothing has to be the way it is; it can all change in a moment, for better and for worse.

When reality breaks, anything is possible. Bread and wine can become the body and blood of a crucified God. The Divine can walk in our midst. Prophets can announce the coming of the glory of the Lord. Sinners can be swept up in the fount of all holiness.

It is the contingency of reality that Christians accept by faith. Nothing has to be the way it is. It is all sustained by the very hand of God. In a moment, one day, God will remake it for good.

And if schizophrenics have just one thing to teach the Church, it is that reality breaks *all the time.*

———

I am not a prophet. In my more lucid moments, that much is clear.

What I am is sick.

And that has made all the difference.

Two

DSM Dreams

As a transgender woman, I am sick in another respect, too.

The psychiatric Scriptures, otherwise known as the fifth edition of the Diagnostic and Statistical Manual of Mental Disorders ("the DSM-5"), specify "Gender Dysphoria in Adolescents and Adults" as,

> A. A marked incongruence between one's experienced/expressed gender and assigned gender, of at least 6 months' duration, as manifested by at least two of the following:

> 1. A marked incongruence between one's experience/expressed gender and primary and/or secondary sex characteristics (or in young adolescents, the anticipated secondary sex characteristics).

> 2. A strong desire to be rid of one's primary and/or secondary sex characteristics because of a marked incongruence with one's experienced/expressed gender (or in young adolescents, a desire to prevent the development of the anticipated secondary sex characteristics).

> 3. A strong desire for the primary and/or secondary sex characteristics of the other gender.

4. A strong desire to be of the other gender (or some alternative gender different from one's assigned gender).

5. A strong desire to be treated as the other gender (or some alternative gender different from one's assigned gender).

6. A strong conviction that one has the typical feelings and reactions of the other gender (or some alternative gender different from one's assigned gender).

B. The condition is associated with clinically significant distress or impairment in social, occupational, or other important areas of functioning.[1]

To say that I meet these criteria is an understatement. The criteria define me.

Death by Gender

Yet it wasn't until I was in my early 20s that I started to identify with them.

I haven't known I was a girl since time immemorial, as some trans women have. But I have known, for as long as I can remember, that my body was fundamentally wrong. Sure, as a child I saw myself most clearly in female fictional characters; and, yes, I tended to adopt female personae when playing make-believe. But at the end of the day, it was the wrongness of my body that caused me to wonder whether I might be trans.

The knowledge came with puberty. I can actually pinpoint the exact moment I first became aware of myself as a sexual being. Because it was the same moment in which I first became aware that my genitalia weren't just incorrect—they needed to go.

I didn't do anything publicly with that knowledge, of course. Growing up in the context of conservative Canadian evangelicalism, I couldn't.

It was only when I broke free of that context, as a master's student at Yale University's School of Divinity in the late 2010s, that I began to seriously probe the nature of my gender discomfort.

Where, previously, I assumed that I simply hated my body, I started to realize that I actually just wanted a different one—a female one. I started to fantasize about inhabiting that different body: I dreamed about it; I imagined the possibilities.

And when I went to bed one night, I prayed—as I had prayed every night before that, for I don't even know how long—that God would transform me, in my sleep, into the woman I wanted so desperately to be. I knew, of course, that God wouldn't. After all, God doesn't seem to be in the business of transforming people from male to female overnight. So I also made myself a promise: come the morning, I would either do something about my "gender problem" or I would kill myself. Either way, I wouldn't be a man anymore.

Subjective Distress and Other Possibilities

What makes gender dysphoria pathological—that is to say, a condition warranting psychiatric attention and intervention—is the "clinically significant distress or impairment" it causes coupled with the persistence of its manifestations over time. That's what makes schizophrenia pathological, too. Indeed, since the introduction of subjective distress and enduring presentation as diagnostic criteria in the DSM-3, that's what makes any psychiatric state a disordered one.[2]

Because there is no necessary connection between psychiatric experiences—even ones as seemingly beyond the pale as hearing voices—and psychological distress. Indeed, a surprising number of people experience what would otherwise be symptoms of mental illness without any associated unease or upset.

Take the hearing voices movement.

Established in the 1980s, the hearing voices movement aims to raise public awareness about the prevalence and diversity of auditory verbal hallucinations ("hearing voices"); to challenge negative stereotypes about those who experience these kinds of hallucinations; and to disseminate strategies for coping with them.[3] At the center of the movement are "voice-hearers" themselves, dubbed "experts by experience" in the phenomenon of hearing voices.[4] And the movement's potential membership is vast: The English "Hearing Voices Network" estimates that anywhere from three percent to ten percent of the population experiences voices, visions, or like sensory phenomena.[5] Other estimates put the prevalence of auditory verbal hallucinations at between four percent and 21 percent, albeit with the caveat that most occurrences of this phenomenon are transient and sporadic rather than sustained.[6] And most of these people simply find ways to cope with their voices and visions, without ever seeking out psychiatric treatment for psychosis.

We can tell a similar story about gender incongruities.

Common sense alone tells us that plenty of people experience "a marked incongruence" between their sex assigned at birth and their gender identity and expression. There is at least as much, if not more, diversity of gender expression within the sexes people are assigned at birth as there is between them.

That is one of the reasons I simply don't buy the common anti-trans talking point that sees radical feminists claiming that, had they been born today, their gender experimentation as young adults would have resulted in them being diagnosed with gender dysphoria. Nor does the idea of "rapid onset" gender dysphoria make much conceptual sense. If the difference between your felt gender and your sex assigned at birth doesn't cause you significant distress or last over time, you don't have gender dysphoria. Full stop.[7]

Be that as it may, there are still good reasons to want to push back against the pathologization of the trans experience. The conditions listed in the DSM-5 are *diseased states* that demand treatments and cures; that hardly seems a fair characterization of the joy a great many trans and gender-diverse people find in their experience of being "born in the wrong bodies." Indeed, in Western societies in which having a mental health diagnosis marks people for flagrant discrimination and abuse, the problem would seem to be more than semantic. As the United States-based National LGBTQ Task Force put it when the DSM-5 was finalized, in 2012:

> As long as gender variance is characterized by the medical field as a mental condition, trans people will find their identities invalidated by claims that they are "mentally ill," and therefore not able to speak objectively about their own identities and lived experiences. This has even been used to justify discrimination against trans people, such as in child custody cases, discrimination in hiring/workplace practices, or justifying them to be mentally unfit to serve in the military.[8]

But what if trans people identified with our disease instead of resisting it?

After the Fall

It is a trite observation indeed to say that the problem Christianity seeks to solve is that of sin, but it is a true one, nonetheless. If there is no sin, Christianity has nothing to do; nothing to offer people; no reason to exist.

I won't attempt a definition of "the problem of sin" just yet. That is, in large respect, the project of this book.

But I will attempt a solution.

When I was still hearing voices, my therapist and I would frequently revisit the question of prognosis. Given that "the devil" was telling me to kill myself; given that "the Illuminati" was pursuing me; given that I could "see" secret messages in the books and articles I read—given all this, what could I reasonably hope for the future?

A lot, it turns out. Although in the depths of psychosis, I could not see it.

My relationship with my hallucinations, in particular, has been an evolving one. As I have come to know them better, I have come to see them as people, too: albeit deeply troubled ones. I started to tell myself that I would no more listen to a voice telling me to hurt myself than I would listen to a stranger telling me the same thing from the other side of the street. On my good days, I even believed that.

I never quite learned to accept and live with my psychotic experiences. Ultimately, I have found the most abiding refuge in their eradication, through high doses of antipsychotic medication and extensive psychotherapy. But on the numerous days when the treatment seemed to be failing and recovery seemed to be out of reach, acceptance was my goal. I wanted to be a voice hearer, not a schizophrenic.

Treatment, in the form of daily hormone therapy and gender-confirming surgery, has likewise provided the most lasting relief from my gender dysphoria. But even now, there are little incongruities between my body and the body of a cisgender female—everything from the way I get my estrogen to the shape of my genitals—that remind me I was not born a woman, I became one. And I often find myself wondering whether I need to make peace with that fact. On my good days, I even do.

What if we could learn to accept sin, too? What if redemption was as much a pedagogy of fallenness as an answer that will one day arrive? What if we could be sinners without fear, without shame, without distress?

That would be cause to hope, too.

Amidst Empty Pews

Following my second year at Yale, I took a summer internship on the Standing Rock Indian Reservation in the Dakotas. My job was to assist the five Episcopal churches on the South Dakota side of the Reservation, and to advise the Episcopal Diocese of South Dakota on church growth strategies. At the time, I thought I wanted to be an Episcopal priest;[9] this position was a dream come true.

Some months before, I had started seeing a therapist who specialized in gender identity issues. We agreed to keep seeing each other virtually while I was in South Dakota. Every Friday, I would slip into an empty church (there was no shortage of them) and talk through my distress at being born male from one or other of the pews.

On one of those Fridays, in late June, we agreed to talk through the DSM-5 criteria for diagnosing gender dysphoria. I had never looked at them before.

Right away, I recognized myself in the criteria. They weren't describing just anyone. They were describing me.

"A diagnosis is comforting because it provides a framework—a community, a lineage—and, if luck is afoot, a treatment or cure."[10] It says that I am not the first person to have had these experiences; that I will not be the last. It says that my condition makes sense. There is a cognitive architecture for understanding what I believed to be inexplicable: the desire to be something other than what I was born.

After we went through the DSM-5 criteria, and I found myself identifying with all of them, I asked my therapist point-blank: "Would you diagnose me with gender dysphoria?" Her response was just as sharp: "Charlotte, I would have diagnosed you with gender dysphoria after our very first appointment together."

Becoming Trans

There is a difference between having gender dysphoria and being trans.

Having gender dysphoria means you are distressed. Being trans means you are doing something about it.

I left my appointment with my therapist and went and sat in a nearby park. It was not long before the tears came, and I started scribbling in my journal.

I knew I needed to transition. And though I did not know, then, exactly how or what transitioning meant, I knew already that transitioning meant experiencing a kind of death. The man I thought I was, the man I thought I had to be, and the troubled future I imagined for that man—all of that would be gone. If I transitioned, I would have to become something new.

Christians might call that conversion.

Three

THE PATHS AHEAD

ONE OF MY EARLIEST memories is of my baptism.

It was Holy Saturday, and there were lots and lots of candles about. The big kind that people hold atop large sticks. You know the type.

I was three or four years old. Which is an odd age to be baptized. Not quite an infant, definitely not an adult. I wasn't baptized because I chose to be; I was baptized because my family wanted it. I was baptized at a little Anglican church nestled deep in the mountains of Western Canada, because that mattered to my family. And, years later, I was confirmed at a little Anglican cathedral on the Western Canadian prairies because that mattered to me.

I remember the day I was born again, too. The first time, anyways. Because growing up conservative evangelical, I had a number of "born again experiences" in which I felt the fire of God descending on me and lighting up my heart from within. But the first time it happened, I was three or four years old. I was attending Sunday school in the basement of the church my family went to. And when the teacher told us kids we could be saved if we just asked Christ into our hearts, I asked her how to do it. She kept me late to tell me; made sure my parents were there, too, when I said that Jesus prayer. I remember it clear as day.

———————

This book is an exercise in Christian theology.

My goal is to take three of the centering points in Christian thought—creation, sin, and redemption—and present them in a coherent whole. As such, there is a narrative cohesion to this project. Its Scriptural focal point is the myth of Eden, and the key problem it considers is the one Christianity tries to solve: human fallenness and its resultant effects.

But this is more than a retelling of the Christian story. It is also an attempt to make sense of *my* story: as a schizophrenic, as a trans woman, and, yes, as someone raised in the Christian faith. The questions this book probes are *my* questions. They are born of my own retrospection on a life of illness and healing, growth and transformation, success and failure. Because theology, in my view, ought to be done in the light of personal experience. After all, if God is to make any sense at all, it is as a God who helps us make sense of what we go through, the ups and the downs of life.

This is a book of memories. It is a story of finding faith, losing it, and in some small way, of finding it again. But it is also a book of questions.

Are schizophrenia and related psychotic illnesses forms of neurodivergence, and what difference does it make for our doctrine of creation? What does it mean for the modern disability rights and feminist movements that the largest psychiatric facilities in North America are prisons, and how should this fact shape our understanding of sin and damnation? What can paranoid delusions tell us about the nature of faith and revelation? How might our theology be shaped by the ongoing abuse crisis plaguing Christian churches, in which 2SLGBTQ+ people are far more likely to be victimized than their non-queer peers?

Each of these questions has something to do with what I've lived through, and with where I am today. My goal, in posing them, is to bring Christianity into dialogue with the key aspects of my life that define my past, present, and future in this world: gender and madness.

A dialogue, by definition, goes two ways. It is a back-and-forth between participants. You get to speak to me but so, too, do I get to speak to you. I get to talk back. Christianity has been talking to me my whole life, in ways big and small, as I'm willing to venture it's been talking to you, too. In this book, I talk back to the faith that raised me, molded me, and in so many ways tried to disown me. *Until At Dawn We Wake* is not just an attempt to make gender and madness make sense in light of key Christian theological categories; it is just as much an attempt to make sense of those same categories in light of my experiences of gender and madness.

My answers to the questions posed above will therefore be personal. They will be reflective of my own, unique circumstances. But I am willing to venture that they will resonate with you in their own way, not least because they might empower you to pose your own questions of the Christian faith tradition and to find your own set of answers. I am willing to venture that my story matters to more than just me.

Now, a word of warning before we proceed. This book is written primarily with Christians in mind. However, I do not write it *as a Christian*. I stopped identifying as such some time ago, and, these days, it is with Reform Jews that I find myself journeying. Each of the chapters that follow registers this shift in its own way. Some of the chapters are quite critical of the Christian tradition, some use Jewish categories to make sense of something in the Christian faith, but none are dismissive of Christianity or its adherents. For Christians will always and evermore be my people, too, if for no other reason than I am who I am because of how Christianity and Christians have shaped me. In the course of this book, reflective as it is of my own wanderings with God, you will see how that is the case.

PART TWO
Creation, Disability

I have heard the voice of God,
sweet like honey.
I have heard the voice of Satan himself,
hard as cold steel.
I have heard the secret whispers
of men no one else can see.
I have heard things no one else believes,
things I cannot believe.

I have seen the faces
of loved ones long departed.
I have seen shapes unfold before me,
the world a kaleidoscope of light.
I have seen people appear before me
and disappear in an instant.
I have seen things no one else believes,
things I cannot believe.

I have felt the ghostly hand of my father
cold upon my shoulder.
I have felt a spectral rope
closing tight around my neck.
I have felt evil itself
in the air around me.
I have felt things no one else believes,
things I cannot believe.

Who are you to say they're not real?
Who am I?

Four

MADNESS, NEURODIVERGENCE

I CANNOT TELL YOU with any certainty when, exactly, I transitioned from the land of the well to the land of the mad. But it was probably sometime during my first year of graduate studies.

It is the delusions that stand out most in retrospect. They crept slowly from the edges of my consciousness into the center. But once they established themselves, I could not shake them.

It began as a general sense of unease about others' intentions. That person who stole a glance at me on the bus? She was watching me. Those colleagues talking in the university quad? They were saying hurtful things about me. That cop driving past me on the street? He was tracking my movements.

And it was this last thought that really took hold, growing into something not unlike an obsession. I was 21 years old, living alone in a country not my own, and every police officer I saw was surveilling me. (This being the United States, of course, there were *a lot* of cops about.) Not only were the police surveilling me, but they were coming to arrest me for some hideous crime. And soon. Which is why, every day, I left my apartment terrified that that would be the day I would be detained and taken away; and why, every day, I would return to my apartment and thoroughly check my door for signs that a police raid was already underway. Some days, I didn't leave my apartment at all, instead barricading myself in my home with the conviction of someone who *just knows* that the very worst is about to happen.

I had committed no crime, of course. In all likelihood, I was far off the radar of any police service. But in the grips of what was, in hindsight, my first episode of psychosis, those facts held no sway.

In the popular imagination, a "psychotic break" is just that: a dramatic rupture in a person's life that comes out of nowhere, forever altering who they are. One moment someone is behaving perfectly normally; the next they're hearing voices, checking their home for listening devices, and babbling incoherently.

The reality, it turns out, is far more complex.

Schizophrenia is an episodic illness. For many people, myself included, it comes and goes with periods of greater symptom intensity interrupted by periods of less.[1] These episodes are often neuroprogressive: each one is damaging to the brain, causing mounting neurological damage as the number of episodes accumulates over the whole of a life.[2] This makes it imperative to intervene as early as possible to disrupt the course of the illness before it can take its full, devastating toll.[3]

It is advantageous, therefore, that psychosis and the psychotic illness schizophrenia almost always begin with something called the prodrome. From the French *prodrome*, which is itself derived from the Classical Latin term *prodromus*, referring to a short book that introduces another, longer one, a prodrome is a precursor or forerunner, a voice that calls out in the wilderness to prepare the way for something else.[4] In schizophrenia, the prodrome is a period of nonspecific, subclinical symptoms that precedes the more dramatic changes in a person that come with the onset of the first psychotic episode. Depression is common during the prodrome, as is anxiety, social isolation, and a general decline in academic and vocational functioning.[5] This period can last anywhere from days, to months, to years.

Unfortunately, however, the prodrome is generally only recognized for what it is—the precursor to psychosis—in retrospect. Its signs and symptoms are so vague, and attributable to so many psychiatric conditions, that if it is treated at all, it is often treated as something else entirely. Which is why, a couple of years before I started listening for approaching footsteps from the other side of my door, I first walked into my doctor's office and asked for a prescription for antidepressants. I was noticing subtle changes, almost imperceptible signs: a felt loss of enjoyment in activities that once brought me joy, a growing sense of alienation from others. The antidepressants worked, to a point—I still take them to stabilize my mood. But they didn't stop the small changes from exploding into the dramatic and alienating experience of full-blown paranoid delusions.

In the end, the antidepressants weren't enough because I was going through something fundamentally different than what they were designed to treat. I was on a trajectory that intersected with depression but ultimately diverged from it. I was on course for madness.

In the Beginning...

The pejorative idea that some people are "mad" and others "sane" is not of recent vintage. "Madness" is one of the curses with which God threatens the Israelites, moments before they enter the Promised Land, should they disobey him (see Deuteronomy 28:28). In the prophet Zechariah's account of a coming siege of Jerusalem, God promises to defend the city by afflicting with madness those who will rise up against it: "'On that day I will strike every horse with panic and its rider with madness,' declares the Lord. 'I will keep a watchful eye over Judah, but I will blind all the horses of the nations'" (Zechariah 12:4 NIV). And in the New Testament, Jesus himself is accused of being "demon-possessed and raving mad" (John 10:20), as if being mad and being an agent of evil, or at least cosmic disorder, were one and the same. There is nothing desirable about madness in the Bible, in other words; it is a scourge to be avoided. And that is reflective of broader societal perceptions of the mad throughout history and into today.

The mad have been villainized, demonized, and hospitalized; shunned, murdered, and oppressed. But as the recently emergent activist field of "mad studies" teaches us, madness can be a term of liberation as well as an object

of fear. The editors of one of the field's foundational texts put it this way in
2013:

> Once a reviled term that signalled the worst kinds of bigotry
> and abuse, madness has come to represent a critical alterna-
> tive to "mental illness" or "disorder" as a way of naming and
> responding to emotional, spiritual, and neuro-diversity. To
> work with and within the language of madness is by no means
> to deny the psychic, spiritual, and material pains and priva-
> tions endured by countless people with histories of encounters
> with the psy disciplines. To the contrary, it is to acknowledge
> and validate these experiences as being authentically human,
> while at the same time rejecting clinical labels that pathologize
> and degrade; challenging the reductionistic assumptions and
> effects of the medical model; locating psychiatry and its hu-
> man subjects within wider historical, institutional, and cul-
> tural contexts; and advancing the position that mental health
> research, writing, and advocacy are primarily about opposing
> oppression and promoting human justice.[6]

Madness, in other words, is the stuff of difference. And that makes it
properly the subject of the doctrine of creation. For difference is the stuff of
creation.

In the beginning, after all, God creates *separation*.

God creates light in order to separate the light from the darkness (Genesis
1:3-4). God creates "the expanse" in order to separate the waters below from
the waters above (Genesis 1:6-7). God creates lights in the expanse in order
to separate the day from the night (Genesis 1:14). In Genesis, creation and
separation go hand-in-hand, so much so that at least one biblical scholar
has suggested the Hebrew word typically translated as "to create" is better
rendered as "to separate."[7] And if that is the case, then God didn't so much

"create" humanity in God's own image, as Genesis 1:27 usually reads; rather, God "separated out" humanity from the rest of creation to bear the image of the Divine.

Of course, the opening chapter of Genesis is a theological myth: a fictitious tale that communicates eternal truths but not scientific facts. I am not disputing that. But I am suggesting that we learn from Genesis 1 that, whatever humanity's evolutionary origins, being different is part of what it means to be created.

And one of the ways difference manifests is through the madness of neurodiversity.

What's in a Name? What's in a Brain?

Neurodiversity is most closely associated with people who experience autism spectrum disorder. As a term, it emerged from "autistic activist communities" operating online in the mid- to late-1990s.[8] The idea was to capture something akin to biodiversity and the fact that everyone's mind and brain differs in important ways.[9] But, over time, the term has spawned a burgeoning body of theoretical and activist work centering those (the neurodiverse) whose brains do not work in the usual fashion (or "neurotypically"). These differences come with advantages and disadvantages, some requiring accommodations by society and some giving the neurodivergent person a leg up on others. But those differences are not "deficits;" they are important and unique ways of being human.[10]

Neurodivergence is not a technical, medical diagnosis. It is an identity that some people have claimed for themselves as a way of asserting and establishing their place in the world. But it is nonetheless based on the observation that people think differently because of biological differences in their neurological wiring. Are those differences present in a psychotic illness like schizophrenia?

The available research says, *yes.*

Psychotic illnesses like schizophrenia seem to be caused by some combination of genetic factors and environmental stressors. That is to say, they are partially inherited and partially induced.[11] Numerous efforts have been made over the years to track the emergence and course of schizophrenia, in particular, in the brain. MRI and postmortem studies alike have shown a decrease in brain matter (particularly gray matter) in people with schizophrenia.[12] Indeed, as psychiatrist Jeffrey Lieberman notes in his summary of the results of decades of functional magnetic resonance imaging of schizophrenic brains,

> In patients with schizophrenia, deficits have been found in several brain regions. These include the dorsolateral prefrontal cortex; anterior cingulate cortex, a structure in the inner part of the frontal cortex involved in mediating higher mental functions, including decision-making, attention focus, and impulse control; and thalamus, a large bundle of neurons sitting on top of the brain stem and midbrain that branch out to the cerebral cortex, transmitting and receiving sensory and motor signals and involved in regulating sleep, arousal, and level of consciousness.[13]

And as other scientists have observed, the greater the number of psychotic episodes a person experiences, and the longer those episodes go untreated, the greater the changes to that person's brain structure.[14] Psychosis, in short, is toxic to the brain.

But those of us who experience psychosis must learn to live with it, and the unique way of inhabiting the world that it represents, all the same. We think differently and require our own set of accommodations; but those differences are not an evil. As one group of scholars put it, the overlap between schizophrenia and autism spectrum disorder is such that they are both "manifestations of neurodiversity stemming from unique cognitive biases. Autistic individuals may overemphasize details and patterns, while schizophrenic individuals might over-attribute intentionality. While potentially maladaptive in contemporary environments, these biases might have held adaptive value in ancestral settings or under specific conditions."[15] I am not in a position to evaluate the evolutionary hypothesis inherent in this claim—that is, that schizophrenia and autism might actually be features human evolution selected *for* in premodern times. But as someone who lives with schizophrenia in the present, I know this much to be true: that schizophrenia confers its own set of benefits, its own set of insights about the world; even as it imposes its own set of demands on the communities I inhabit.

Neurodivergent, not "High-Functioning"

There's a perverse rationality to my psychosis.

It begins as whispers on the wind. A voice calling my name. Demonic faces appearing and then vanishing. A man narrating my thoughts and actions wherever I go.

Strange interpretations follow from strange experiences.

I have a divine mission, like a prophet of old. How else can I explain the omnipresent demonic legions haunting my steps?

To exist on the schizophrenia spectrum as I do—in the company of those with schizoaffective disorder; schizophreniform disorder; other specified and unspecified schizophrenia spectrum disorders; and, of course, schizophrenia itself—is to exist differently than those whose minds do not venture so easily into the realm of the unreal. It is to know the world differently, as a scarier yet more spellbinding place. Indeed, it is to *be* different than those without psychotic experience.

But most days these days you would not know I have an illness so horrifying some psychiatrists withhold the diagnosis from their patients for fear of triggering anxiety and despair.[16] You would not know I am a mad woman.

That's because, most days these days, I have schizophrenia: *But...* I have schizophrenia: But I don't usually talk to myself in public. I have schizophrenia: But I'm usually pretty good about hiding my delusions. I have schizophrenia: But it's well-managed. I have schizophrenia: But I can generally keep up with work and school, feed myself, and maintain my hygiene.

I have schizophrenia: But by the usual measures of psycho-social functioning—ability to hold a job, continue with schooling, maintain interpersonal relationships, and maintain my general well-being—I am a "high-functioning" schizophrenic.

It is a label some who share my diagnostic label wear with pride,[17] all the more so in recent years as more and more people have come forward to share their stories of being both successful and schizophrenic. After all, advocates say, schizophrenics can be lawyers, businesspeople, and teachers—anything we want to be—provided we receive the proper combination of treatment and support. Give us the right antipsychotics, teach us to challenge our hallucinations and delusions with rational thought, make sure we're getting a good night's sleep, and you'll see: we're not so different from everyone else.

But a person with "high functioning" schizophrenia is still on the schizophrenia spectrum. And that's the rub: it *does* make us different.

I will live with my illness for the rest of my life—there is no cure. And that means I will have to work every day to maintain my grasp on the real world; knowing that even if I take my medications, spend hour after hour in psychotherapy, and am diligent about applying the skills I have learned to manage my symptoms, my hold on reality will still slip every now and again.

Whether because of stress or the capriciousness of fate, my madness will strike again.

"High functioning" implies normalcy, remission, and recovery—when what I have is an illness that sometimes requires more support, sometimes less, but that is ever present.

I can be high functioning one day and low functioning the next. I can be high functioning in some ways and low functioning in others. But regardless of the day or the way, I exist on the schizophrenia spectrum. That's never going to change.

In fact, I have more in common with my "low functioning" siblings on the schizophrenia spectrum than I do with people who do not share my illness at all. Where the "high functioning" label suggests that I am somehow differ-ent—better, even—than them, I see commonality. I, too, know what it's like to lose touch with the real world. To be plagued by the hallucinations and delusions that are caricatured in Hollywood depictions of our illness—and by the cognitive and emotional deficits that aren't so easily portrayed. To fear what the medical system will do—involuntary admissions, restraints, locked rooms—when its powers to heal fail. Above all, that reality is a gift not easily regained once lost.

I know what law professor Elyn Saks captured so poignantly in her power-ful memoir of a life defined by the experience of psychosis and schizophrenia, namely, that

> Dropping in and out of your own life (for psychotic breaks, or treatment in a hospital) isn't like getting off a train at one stop and later getting back on at another. Even if you can get back on (and the odds are not in your favor), you're lonely there. The people you boarded with originally are far, far ahead of you, and now you're stuck playing catch-up.[18]

A World of Difference

I might not be able to tell you when, exactly, the delusions started. But I can tell you exactly when I was officially diagnosed as having schizophrenia. It was an autumn day some years after I first became convinced the police were about to kick down my front door and execute a search warrant; some years after I first started counting the number of white cars parked on my street, convinced that every one of them was evidence of an Illuminati plot (but more on that later); some years after I first heard the voices that would torment me.

I was already unwell by the time I received my diagnosis. And that is, of course, the nature of diagnoses: they come after an illness has already made its presence felt in your life. By the time you're diagnosed, you're already sick.

But my psychiatrist, in assigning my particular package of symptoms the name of "schizophrenia," was doing more than just making me "officially" ill. He wasn't just separating me out from the healthy, that is to say, from the people who aren't psychotic. He was including me in something, too; something much bigger than myself. He was giving me an identity amongst the mad. What I was experiencing was neither random nor senseless. It had a name, a history, and a future. And that name, that history, that future—they were mine, too.

Diagnoses evidence a simple fact about the created world: division and separation are the prerequisites for inclusion.[19] In order to be included in something, we cannot already be a part of it. We must be different, in some fundamental way.

And in the beginning, it was God who separated out the creatures in our differences: "God made the wild animals according to their kinds, the livestock according to their kinds, and all the creatures that move along the ground according to their kinds. And God saw that it was good" (Genesis 1:25).

The language of neurodiversity helps us make sense of the divine conclusion that the diversity of created beings is *good*.

To invoke that language is to do more than make the trite biological observation that different people think differently. It is to do more, even, than make the statement that there is value in different ways of thinking, indeed, in different ways of inhabiting the created world. (Although it is certainly not to do less than those things.) It is to assert as a matter of fact that the prerequisite has been satisfied for accommodating, including, and welcoming those differences. It is to make *community* possible.

In arguing that schizophrenia is a form of neurodivergence, I am not idealizing psychosis or any other experience that falls under the collective umbrella of neurodiversity. Our differences come with difficulties, too: for us as well as for those around us who might have to accommodate our needs. I know that all too well. But recognizing and working within those difficulties is part and parcel of being inclusive.

Inclusion, after all, is a tricky project. It demands much of those of us who would pursue it.

Five

DISABILITY AND THE SEVENTH DAY

CREATION CULMINATES, NOT IN labor, but in rest.

For six days, Genesis teaches, God worked: separating the land from the sea, commanding the earth to sprout vegetation, and forging humanity in God's own image. And when God saw all that God had made, God "found it very good" (Genesis 1:31 JPS). But on the seventh day, God "ceased from all the work of creation;" therefore "God blessed the seventh day and declared it holy" (Genesis 2:3).

What is this Sabbath, this *Shabbat*, that God sanctified on the seventh day?

Our guide, in probing this question, is Abraham Joshua Heschel. Among the leading Jewish theologians of the 20th century, *The Sabbath* was his meditation on the meaning and significance of the seventh day. A monumental work of spiritual and devotional reflection, the book, originally published in 1951, continues to guide Christian as well as Jewish readers grappling with the meaning of *Shabbat* for modern people.

To encounter *Shabbat*, Heschel writes, is to step into Judaism's "great cathedrals,"[1] its "palace in time."[2] For *Shabbat* is what completes creation as well as what precedes it.[3] Before God began to create the heavens and the earth, before God swept over the water and formed light out of pure breath—before every *thing*, God rested. *Shabbat* is a small piece of that original rest embedded in the architecture of creation itself; it "is all of the spirit that the world can bear."[4]

What does it mean to rest in a world obsessed with labor? Put differently, in phrasing truer to Heschel's own framing of the question: What does it mean to sanctify time in a world obsessed with acquiring space?

"Technical civilization," Heschel writes, "is man's conquest of space. It is a triumph frequently achieved by sacrificing an essential ingredient of existence, namely, time. *In technical civilization, we expend time to gain space.*"[5]

Space, here, is a synecdoche for all the things of life. It stands in for the whole—for the living and the dying, for the planting and the uprooting, for the weeping and the laughing, for the keeping and the discarding, for the silence and the speaking, for the warring and the peacemaking, and for all those other tasks, so eloquently poeticized by the author of Ecclesiastes, that make up human existence.[6]

But time stands for itself: It "has independent ultimate significance."[7]

And that is the key distinction. Space is divisible; time is eternal. "Time is the process of creation, and things of space are results of creation."[8] Space is something people can own; time is something people necessarily share, with each other and with God.

The problem inherent to what Heschel calls "technical civilization"—but what we might just as easily call "capitalism" or, more generally, "modernity"—is that it confuses the means of life, space, with the ends of life, time. Acquisition and ownership become the goal; time is "spent" to attain them.

That is because, in the neoliberal moment we presently inhabit here in North America, capitalism disciplines the bodies and minds of we its subjects to be always oriented towards work.

I find Wendy Brown's treatment of the vague and nebulous concept of "neoliberalism" insightful. "Neoliberal rationality," she writes, "disseminates the *model of the market* to all domains and activities—even where money is not at issue—and configures human beings exhaustively as market actors, always, only, and everywhere as *homo oeconomicus*."[9] What Brown means is that market logics have come to define human decision-making even in those circumstances where the market is seemingly absent. Thus, for example, people make such decisions as which social media platforms to use, which universities to attend and for what, even which books to read and which clothes to wear in terms of the returns on investment that those decisions will yield. Not just financially, but also in terms of emotional returns, interpersonal returns (in the form of "influence" over others), and so forth. And the reason for this constant, complex, but mostly subconscious calculus is that, under neoliberalism, people are capital in our own right. *We* are investment products, rigorously disciplined to ensure everything we do increases our value as *human capital*.[10] The goal of life is to increase the worth of our "personal brand," and that means *always working*.

For Heschel, toil—enslavement to work—is the problem.[11] *Shabbat* is the solution: "a day on which we would not use the instruments which have been so easily turned into weapons of destruction, a day for being with ourselves, a day of detachment from the vulgar, of independence of external obligations, a day on which we stop worshipping the idols of technical civilization, a day on which we use no money, a day of armistice in the economic struggle with our fellow men and the forces of nature."[12]

Shabbat is a place, constructed within time, to which everyone is called. "The seventh day," Heschel writes, "is like a palace in time with a kingdom for all. It is not a date but an atmosphere."[13] Where the things of space are "good," the time of *Shabbat* is "holy."[14] Six days out of every week we labor; on the seventh day we rest.

Rest here is total. On *Shabbat*, we are all of us commanded to "rest even from the thought of labor."[15]

The reason is that *Shabbat* is eternity made manifest.[16] "The essence of the world to come is Sabbath eternal, and the seventh day in time is an example of eternity."[17] *Shabbat* reminds us that creation is finished, that God has already completed that good work; and it reminds us, too, that when the things of creation are over, at the End of Days, all that will remain is to rest, to *sanctify time*. "This is the task of men: to conquer space and sanctify time... All week long we are called upon to sanctify life through employing things of space. On the Sabbath it is given us to share in the holiness that is the heart of time."[18]

All of creation, and the whole of our lives as created beings, is a buildup to *Shabbat*. And therein lies the point. For to encounter *Shabbat* is to encounter disability each and every week.

Religious Disabilities

Jewish law identifies 39 categories of work that are prohibited on *Shabbat*. Banned is everything from plowing to threshing to baking to building to kindling to writing.[19] The categories themselves derive from the tasks that were necessary for the building of the Tabernacle, described in the Book of Exodus. And for *Shabbat*-observant Jews, work does indeed cease on the seventh day.

This has real-life consequences for those Jews' participation in the contemporary marketplace. They cannot work shifts on Saturdays, for example; make purchases on that day; or even, in Orthodox and Orthodox-adjacent Jewish traditions, engage in such simple tasks as flipping a light switch.

In short, the *Shabbat*-observant Jew is disabled one day a week.

To say this is merely to be attuned to the practical implications of keeping this religious holiday. A person who makes *Shabbat* can no more work on a Saturday than I could when the hallucinations and delusions were at their most incapacitating. Indeed, society must make accommodations if either the *Shabbat*-observant Jew or I the schizophrenic are to be able to participate in public life. And, in some limited cases, that is exactly what happens.

The rules governing *Shabbat* observance include a prohibition on carrying items outside of one's home. To permit people to push strollers and carry housekeys, some cities with large Orthodox Jewish communities have therefore installed *eruvin*—thin wires suspended above the ground that symbolically extend the boundaries of people's homes into what is ostensibly the public sphere.[20]

This is a form of state-sponsored religious accommodation, a way of including Orthodox Jews in the life of the city on Judaism's holiest day. But it is one that illustrates the tensions inherent to the project of inclusion.

In 2000, the City of Outremont, Québec, began to dismantle the *eruvin* installed above its streets and sidewalks, citing its duty not to discriminate. One of the City's arguments was that "the erection of *eruvin* involuntarily place non-members of the Orthodox Jewish faith within what amounts to a religious enclave with which they do not wish to be associated."[21] The *eruvin* were, in other words, too inclusive, capturing within their ambit people who did not want anything to do with Orthodox Judaism. Removing Outremont's system of *eruvin* was thus a way of including the members of other faiths by excluding those Orthodox Jews on *Shabbat*.

Religious difference, in a modern multicultural society like Canada, is tolerated "only so long as it is not *so different* that it challenges the organizing norms, commitments, practices, and symbols of the Canadian constitutional rule of law."[22] That's the point legal scholar Benjamin Berger makes in *Law's Religion*, a study of Canadian religious and legal cultures. What Berger means is that the tolerated religious practice is the legally "acceptable" one. The rule of law brooks no rivals, and, thus, "the more that a given religious culture or practice accords with law's understanding of religion, the less abrasive and challenging to law's commitments it will be and, hence, the more likely it is that it will fall within the limits of legal tolerance. When, however, a claim to religious freedom begins to grate or put pressure on the law, it appears legally intolerable."[23] So, for example, it is all well and good to insist on not carrying keys on Saturdays; that is a personal decision (the bread and butter of liberal rights discourse) that makes few demands on public life. But it is something else entirely to demand that others within your town or city, say, participate in your religious observance.

We can perform a similar analysis of the physical impairments that constitute the biological facts, as it were, of contemporary disability politics. Disabled bodies, be they governed by the *Americans with Disabilities Act of 1990* ("the *ADA*")[24] or Canadian human rights laws, must be impaired *in the right ways* to qualify as such. It is not enough merely to have a psychiatric disorder under the *DSM*, say. If it were, trans people would qualify for disability protections on the basis of our gender dysphoria. But we do not.

Disability Beyond the Pale

The "moral code" of contemporary disability politics, in the United States at least, is the *ADA*; and trans people are "its moral castaways."[25] That's the assessment of legal scholar Kevin Barry. The *ADA* is a comprehensive piece of civil rights legislation that protects disabled people from discrimination in various facets of life, including employment and access to government services. But—and this is Barry's point—in the moral imagination of the *Act*, not all disabilities are created equal. Trans people, notably, find ourselves in disturbing company.

"Disability" in the unamended, original text of the legislation means any of three things. First, "a physical or mental impairment that substantially limits one or more of [a person's] major life activities." Second, "a record of such an impairment." Or, third, "being regarded as having such an impairment."[26]

Not every aspect of human difference rises to the level of an impairment, however. And for clarity the *Act* specifies that gay and bisexual folks do not suffer an impairment on account of their sexual orientation.[27] So far so good for the project of de-stigmatizing queer identities.

But then a funny thing happens. The *ADA* goes on to name some things that, although no doubt impairments, are too far beyond the pale to warrant disability rights protections:

Under this Act, the term 'disability' shall not include

(1) transvestism, transsexualism, pedophilia, exhibitionism, voyeurism, gender identity disorders not resulting from physical impairments, or other sexual behavior disorders;

(2) compulsive gambling, kleptomania, or pyromania; or

(3) psychoactive substance use disorders resulting from current illegal use of drugs.[28]

With a stroke of a pen, the *ADA* drives a stake between the "LGB" and the
"T." Unlike the former, the latter suffer from an impairment, to be sure; but
they are "'too disabled' to be rehabilitated into citizenship, or not properly
disabled enough to be recoded for labor productivity."[29]

Now, it will not be surprising to anyone who has inhabited a trans body
for any length of time that the *ADA* conceives of gender dysphoria (in its
pre-DSM-V terminology, "gender identity disorders") as akin to pedophilia.
One of the more common refrains of those opposed to gender diversity in
North American public life is that trans people are "grooming" children for
sexual abuse merely by existing. But if it is one thing to have one's gender
identity likened in online discourse to the proclivities of sexual predators, it
is another thing entirely to read such a comparison in United States federal
legislation. For starters, the latter enshrines into law a governmental refusal
to extend anti-discrimination protections to people like oneself.

The historical reason for that refusal was primarily moral. When the
ADA made its way through Congress, in 1989, Republican Senator William
Armstrong of Colorado objected that he "could not imagine the sponsors
would want to provide a protected legal status to somebody who has such
[mental] disorders, particularly those [that] might have a moral content to
them or which in the opinion of some people have a moral content."[30]
Armstrong meant everything from "alcohol withdrawal," to "hallucinosis
[*sic*]," to "marijuana" use.[31] Other Republican senators pressed Armstrong's
objection, demanding to know how the *ADA* could protect not only "people
in a wheelchair" but also "transvestites."[32] And a version of that objection
won the day, as we have already seen, such that "the ADA became, in effect,
a moral code: 'disability' coverage applies to those we pity, not those we
despise."[33]

When the *ADA* was amended, in 2008, Congress "expand[ed] the definition of 'disability'...to include nearly everyone."[34] No longer does one need to meet strict and narrow judicial interpretations of "substantial" limits on "major life activities" to qualify for federal protections. Now it is enough to show that one was "discriminated against (e.g., fired, not hired) based on an impairment."[35] And "because everyone has an impairment of one sort or another (or may be perceived as having one), this means that everyone, with only a few exceptions, is entitled to legal protection."[36] Experiencing an ankle injury, bipolar disorder, obesity, or stuttering? You have a case under the revamped *ADA* that you are disabled.[37]

But the exclusionary paragraphs from the original legislation were retained. Indeed, the only forms of human difference that do not qualify for disability rights protection would seem to be the moral "depravities" that were excluded from the *ADA*'s original definition of disability. For the amended *Act* continues to place "transsexualism" and "gender identity disorders not resulting from physical impairments" together with "pedophilia," "pyromania," and other troubling proclivities beyond the ambit of its definition of "disability."

To understand why, we will need to get our terminology straight.

In contemporary theorizations of "disability," a strong distinction is often drawn between it and an impairment.[38] The latter is any deviation from the biological "norm" in a person's physical or mental state; the former are all the exclusions that society imposes upon people who deviate in that fashion.[39]

Put aside the question of whether gender dysphoria is an impairment or a disability for a moment. My schizophrenia is undoubtedly disabling on the *ADA*'s terms; we'll use that as our example to make the impairment versus disability distinction clear.

I cannot pinpoint with any accuracy the earliest manifestations of my psychiatric impairments. They likely started up during my graduate studies, when the paranoia began to creep into the corners of my thinking. They were undoubtedly present later when I experienced my first hallucinations of the "Shadow Man," as I called the indistinct figure who stalked my waking hours.

But I do know when I first became disabled on account of my schizophrenia. It was a chilly February morning, partway through my fourth semester of law school, when I finally admitted what university administrators and medical professionals had been urging me to recognize for some time: my impairment had become such that I could not continue with life as I knew it. Something had to change.

In the brutally practical terms of the modern university, that meant taking a leave of absence from my course of studies. Maybe I could still become a lawyer, but not yet. My impairment had exceeded the limits of what the university was prepared to accommodate.

In the theoretical terms of the "social model of disability," I had become disabled.

Coined by Michael Oliver in 1981,[40] the social model has long been favored by disability scholars and activists as preferable to medical models of disability that locate disability in the physical and mental "defects" of individuals.[41] It instead posits disability as a failure of social inclusion. Under this approach, schizophrenia rendered me impaired. But the fact that my social groups responded to that impairment by excluding me from the activities I wanted to join in on—going to school, for one—rendered me disabled.

Now, it is no exaggeration to say that becoming disabled saved my life, in no small part because it afforded me a socially legitimate way of engaging in extended rest. And therein lies the rub: In the United States and Canada, to become "disabled" is to *gain* access to certain benefits *as disabled*. Most basically, the disabled body is one that, on paper at least, cannot be discriminated against—even if the comprehensive wording of legislation like the *ADA* implies that the disabled body is one that will *always* be discriminated against, hence the need for expansive anti-discrimination laws. And the disabled body is in many respects exempt from the neoliberal drive to always work.

What, then, do we do with the fact that some bodies experience impairments but do not qualify as disabled? More bluntly: What do we do with trans bodies?

Critical theorist Jasbir Puar writes of "debility" as a liminal category that transcends the dichotomy of "ability" and "disability" without being reducible to either. "While some bodies may not be recognized as or identify as disabled," Puar writes in a theoretical description of what I have just said, "they may well be debilitated, in part by being foreclosed access to legibility and resources as disabled. Relatedly, some bodies may well be disabled but also capacitated."[42] Debility, on this analysis, is neoliberalism's collateral damage. It is the injury that neoliberalism neither has to justify nor remedy. And that injury manifests, in part, as the denial of protections and state services.

By this definition, trans bodies are debilitated but not disabled. Their exclusion from the legislative protections of the *ADA* is such that they are the bodies society has every right to exclude. This makes them *socially disabled*—in the framing of the social model of disability, a marginalized group—but, legally speaking, in the wrong ways.

Choosing Debility

On one accounting of things, disability and labor are polar opposites. The bodies and minds that are fit to work are able; the bodies and minds that are not are disabled; and everyone fits into one or the other category, but never both.

It would be truer to the human experience, however, to speak of disability and labor as partners, ever co-mingling and never truly opposed. And here, again, Heschel's meditation on *Shabbat* is instructive. "The Sabbath as a day of abstaining from work," he writes, "is not a depreciation but an affirmation of labor, a divine exaltation of its dignity. Thou shalt abstain from labor on the seventh day is a sequel to the command: *Six days shalt thou labor, and do all thy work*."[43] There is, in other words, fulfillment—spiritual and otherwise—to be found in labor, but this is so to the extent that people can attain independence from their tasks.

Shabbat asserts that independence.[44] Although it comes at a cost.

Shabbat, Heschel says, is "a day of independence of social conditions."[45] What he means is that *Shabbat* is available equally to all, regardless of one's economic means or degree of study. But we might just as easily say that *Shabbat* manifests neoliberalism's social inequalities, indeed, that it amplifies them. For in choosing to make *Shabbat*, people choose to be excluded from the marketplace and its unrelenting drive to never stop working. They choose to be marginal.

And that choice is everything.

To have a "disability," Puar tells us in her definition of the term, you must be "that body or that subject that can aspire both economically and emotionally to wellness, empowerment, and pride through the exceptionalized status it accrues while embedded within unexceptional and, in fact endemic, debility."[46] In other words, your debility needs to make sense *as a disability* to the government and the rest of society. And gender dysphoria doesn't any more than pedophilia or kleptomania.

That's because disability can't be a choice. It has to be something that fate has inflicted upon you. It has to be an unfortunate turn of events—one in which you had no say, because, if you did, you would necessarily have opted for things to turn out differently. For disability, in the moral reasoning of the neoliberal marketplace, is *bad*.

But while you might not have any say over whether you experience an incongruence between your felt gender and the sex you were assigned at birth, you certainly have a choice about whether to do anything about that psychiatric fact. Gender dysphoria might be an affliction; but "transsexualism," changing your sex, is a decision. And no one in their right mind would choose that.

But where the marketplace says that ability is good and disability bad, *Shabbat* says that all bodies and all minds are first and foremost made to rest; that the social exclusion that attaches to disability is desirable in its own way. To choose *Shabbat* is to choose disability each and every week. It is to look upon rest, and the exclusion rest necessarily entails, not as *good*, but as something higher: as *holy*.

Holiness, after all, means separation. It means being different. Whether it is a person, a place, or a thing: when something is "holy" (in Hebrew: *qadosh*), it is "set apart" for a specific, Divine purpose. And holiness in the Hebrew Bible is a matter of *doing* things in order to *be* different. In Leviticus 19:2, at the beginning of what scholars call the "Holiness Code," God tells Moses to command the Israelites to "be holy, for I, the Lord your God, am holy." From what follows, the Israelites learn that, to be holy, they must act in specific ways to distinguish themselves from the nations. Keeping *Shabbat—disabling themselves—*is one of those things.[47]

And, Genesis tells us, the person who makes *Shabbat* first and foremost is none other than Godself.

Does this mean, then, that God is ultimately disabled, too?

Sustaining Rest

"The disabled God," writes Nancy Eiesland in her seminal theology of disability, "is God for whom interdependence is not a possibility to be willed from a position of power, but a necessary condition for life."[48] God *needs* people; not in an abstract sense, but in a corporeal, embodied one. God needs the care that people can provide, and thus depends in a very real way on sustaining a relationship with God's own creation.

Beginning in Exodus 25, God gives the Israelites encamped in the wilderness of Sinai instructions for constructing the Tabernacle. "Let [the Israelites] make Me a sanctuary that I may dwell among them," God tells Moses in Exodus 25:8. There is to be a physical place in the midst of the camp, which the Divine presence will inhabit. And, in what follows, Moses—to say nothing of Exodus' readers—learn in painstaking detail what steps the Israelites need to take, indeed what accommodations they need to make, in order for that to be possible.

It would have been both easier and safer for God to make the Divine home in heaven. But God chooses, instead, to make it among people. In so doing, God throws God's lot in with the children of Israel. Their camp's security and success will be God's own security and success. Their accommodation of God's needs, in the form of adherence to the *mitzvoth* (commandments) of Torah, will ensure the possibility of God's continued presence amongst them.

The disabled God is one who suffers when God's people suffer. The disabled God is one who leaves the sanctuary of holy places when God's people make a mockery of God's laws, as the prophet Ezekiel relates so vividly in his vision of the Divine presence abandoning the First Temple just prior to its destruction in 587/86 BCE at the hands of the Babylonian armies.[49] The disabled God is one who is present only so long as we make space for God to dwell amongst us.

And all of this is because God chose it to be so.

Underlying the idea that disability cannot be a choice is the notion that human difference itself is a tragedy. But it is not.[50] The fact that some people are seeing and others are not; the fact that some people walk and others do not; the fact that some people hallucinate and others never do—these are not problems to be solved. Rather, they are aspects of the human experience to be embraced.

I don't say that lightly. I have often wondered whether I would have opted for the hallucinations and the delusions and the paranoia that have so defined my life these past few years had God given me the choice to experience psychosis or not. That question will always remain hypothetical, of course, for I had no such choice. I did, however, have an opportunity to choose whether to transition my gender; I make that choice every single day that I elect to live as a woman. And it is one that I make *knowing* that it comes with social exclusion and marginalization.

I choose debility. Just as, at sundown each Friday, I choose to make *Shabbat*. Because the choice itself is holy.

PART THREE
Sin, Detention

Sitting on my best friend's bathroom floor, the lights off and the door closed, staring into the darkness. Before me, a kaleidoscope of color and moving shapes. Without hearing a word, I know I am looking into hell.

Lying on my bed reading the Gospel of John. My dad makes me read it when I've misbehaved.

The shadowy silhouette of a man, standing maybe a block away. He follows me home that night, but I never see him move.

The lines of the topless woman before me. The feel of her skin against mine. The reassurances she gives me. I'm 9. I don't remember how old she is.

Seeing my dad's face in the car we just drove past. In the stone of my kitchen island. In my nightmares. He's been dead 7 years now.

My cat snuggled up next to me, purring in his sleep and content as can be.

Scouring my apartment for microphones. Keeping my voice low when I talk on the phone. I know they're somewhere. I heard them being installed last night.

Huddled in the middle of a dark room, staring at the door, praying my dad doesn't walk through it. If he does, he'll kill me. I'm 6.

"Their voices are many, for they are legion." Maybe a pentagram will keep these demons at bay.

The slow realization that working with my hands makes the voices go away.

The psychiatrist telling me I have no choice but to spend the night in the emergency room. No, they don't know what illness afflicts me. I'm sobbing so hard my nose starts to bleed. I'm 25 and have never felt so alone.

The way his hands grab my ankles as he pushes into me. The way I cry out in pain. The way nothing makes him stop.

Standing on a hill overlooking the prairies after sundown. The lights of distant farmhouses shimmering before me like so many stars.

The warm embraces we've shared.

Six

The Valley of the Shadow
of Death

At Port-Cartier Institution in northern Québec, guards twisted Nicholas Dinardo's arm behind their back with such force that they broke it—an incident from May 30, 2021, that even Correctional Service Canada ("CSC") recognizes was an excessive and disproportionate use of violence.[1] This is one of the few occasions in which violence against a person imprisoned in a Canadian carceral institution has been reported publicly.

More common are the unreported stories provided to me by incarcerated people themselves and their legal advocates. Stories like that of Alexa, who was incarcerated in a federal penitentiary over a decade ago and alleges that guards would let others into her cell to rape her. Or that of Darla, incarcerated in another of Canada's federal penitentiaries, who alleges that she was sexually assaulted in her cell by fellow inmates, some of whom stood watch at the door for passing guards. In order to protect the safety of these and other incarcerated trans, nonbinary, and Two-Spirit people, I have agreed to grant them pseudonyms and not to publish the names of their institutions or the offences of which they were convicted.

The fact is, trans, nonbinary, and Two-Spirit people held in Canadian federal custody (i.e., those serving sentences of two years or longer[2]) face violence and injustice on a daily basis. The government's discriminatory policies are only making matters worse.

There were 99 openly trans, nonbinary, and Two-Spirit people in federal custody when CSC last published data on its gender-diverse inmate population, in 2022.[3] Of those, 62 percent identified as trans women and 21 percent

as trans men. The vast majority were housed in institutions that correspond-
ed with their birth sex rather than their gender identity: 67 percent of trans
women were housed in men's institutions, and 95 percent of trans men were
housed in women's institutions.

Amy Matychuk practices prison law in Calgary, Alberta. She currently
represents about five percent of the trans women in Canadian federal custody. Matychuk says that the reason why most trans women are housed in
men's institutions is that CSC keeps finding an "overriding health and safety
concern" to keep them there.

The issue, you see, is CSC policy.

In June 2017, the Government of Canada amended the *Canadian Human Rights Act* to explicitly prohibit discrimination on the basis of "gender
identity" and "gender expression."[4] CSC responded later that year by enact-
ing an interim policy for managing gender diversity in federal institutions.
That policy was finalized in 2022 as *Commissioner's Directive 100: Gender
Diverse Offenders.*[5]

The directive specifies that, at intake, "offenders will be placed according
to their gender identity or expression in a men's or a women's institution, if
that is their preference, regardless of their sex (i.e., anatomy) or the gender/sex
marker on their identification documents. In the event there are overriding
health or safety concerns that cannot be resolved, the offender will be placed
in a site that better aligns with their current sex (i.e., anatomy)."

Likewise, during the course of their sentence, people may voluntarily
transfer to an institution that better aligns with their gender identity. But
this, too, is subject to "health or safety concerns" and approval by either the
Assistant Commissioner for Correctional Operations and Programs (when
applying for a transfer to a men's institution) or the Deputy Commissioner
for Women (when applying for a transfer to a women's institution).

"In my experience," Matychuk says, "these transfer requests are frequently
denied ... and almost every application to transfer from a men's to a women's
prison that I've seen has been denied on the grounds of health and safety
concerns." The data bears this observation out. In practice, CSC has used

the Overriding Health and Safety Provision in *Commissioner's Directive 100* to deny 83 percent of the trans women in its custody transfers to women's carceral institutions.[6]

The deciding factor, Matychuk has found, is a person's genitalia.

Megan's Story

Megan has been in federal custody for more than 25 years.

She's known she was a woman since she was ten. But when she was incarcerated at 21 years old, she knew prison was "not a safe space" in which to come out and disclose her gender identity.

Other trans women in the men's system suffered "the most horrible abuse not only from their fellow inmates, but also from staff," Megan tells me, and that "entrenched me into my closet even more."

It was only after she began to process her own trauma—including the trauma of going through male puberty—that Megan began to come out of that closet.

In 2018, she came out to her case-management team as "gender neutral" and was met with significant confusion. "Most staff didn't know what the hell to do with me," she says. There were questions about why she was only coming out now, and how this news related to risk management, she says.

A few months later, Megan officially started identifying as a woman, adopted she/her pronouns, and came out to others housed in the men's institution she was in.

"Almost from day one," she says, "I had to start filing complaints to get my basic gender needs met."

Staff made no effort to use her pronouns or to respect her search protocols. "If you want special privileges in a prison, [transitioning] is not the way to go about it," she reflects.

In 2019, she alleges, a male correctional officer sexually assaulted her during a search. CSC considered it merely a policy violation.

Megan applied for a transfer to a women's institution on three different occasions and was denied each time despite being a minimum-security inmate with no institutional charges.

In 2022, after fighting CSC for access for over a year, she received breast augmentation. Her augmented breasts triggered a lot of unwanted attention and harassment from fellow inmates. Two of them cornered and sexually assaulted her. Megan had to physically fight her way out. One of the alleged perpetrators later confessed to the assault; CSC kept him in Megan's unit.

Megan was scheduled to receive gender-confirming vaginoplasty later that year at GrS Montreal, until recently the only place in Canada to receive male-to-female bottom surgery.[7]

Three days before her surgery was scheduled to take place, she received a phone call from her parole officer. The Deputy Commissioner for Women still hadn't decided whether to allow Megan into a women's institution post-vaginoplasty. She had to decide for herself whether to go through with the surgery and risk going to a men's institution afterward, or to postpone it and live with the mental health challenges of ongoing dysphoria.

"I don't know if you can even fathom how terrifying that was for me," she says. Were her transfer request to be denied again, "the threat of rape would have been constant."

She decided to go forward with her surgery anyway. Thirty minutes before it was scheduled to take place, she found out she would be transferred to a women's institution afterward.

It was a "gigantic relief," she says.

Discrimination by any Other Name

Prisoners' Legal Services ("PLS") is a clinic in the Western Canadian province of British Columbia that provides legal aid to people incarcerated in that province.

They tell me that "out of 47 requests by gender-diverse individuals for placement or transfer to institutions designated for women ... only seven (or

15 percent) were approved, while 34 (or 72 percent) were denied (another six were either withdrawn or pending)."

Nicole Kief is a policy director and senior legal advocate at PLS. In her experience, transphobia saturates CSC's approach to managing the trans, nonbinary, and Two-Spirit people in its custody.

Dinardo is a PLS client who identifies as a Two-Spirit transfeminine person. Since coming out, Kief says, "they've spent most of their time in 'structured intervention units,' which are ... basically like another form of isolation." CSC, she says, "has refused to transfer them to an institution designated for women and relied on transphobic stereotypes in making those decisions."

Those sorts of stereotypes saw the light of day in *Boulachanis v Canada (Attorney General)*,[8] a 2019 Federal Court decision that granted Jamie Boulachanis a transfer to a women's institution. In opposing Boulachanis's transfer application, the federal government relied heavily on the transphobic myth that "the escape risk of a person with male anatomy, even though she identifies as a woman and is transitioning to become a woman, can be different simply by virtue of her physical capabilities and muscular strength associated with her male chromosomes." The court rejected that argument, and the biological determinism on which it rests, as "discriminatory prejudice." But it's an argument that continues to underlie CSC policy and decision-making.

CSC refuses to change a person's sex designation in their electronic Offender Management System unless that person undergoes gender-confirming bottom surgery;[9] which means that a pre-operative trans person's sex assigned at birth appears in the header of every official document relating to them, effectively outing them to decision-makers and exposing them to discrimination. Transfeminine people in men's institutions are put in men's programming, Kief explains, and CSC then uses the fact that they haven't done appropriate programming to deny their transfer to a women's institution. And CSC routinely uses factors like a trans person's "high mental health needs" to deny them a transfer.

All of this is despite the fact that CSC would never house a cis woman in a men's institution for these same reasons, no matter the health, safety or programming concerns.

No Utopias

Of course, even when trans women *are* transferred to women's institutions, Kief says, there's this idea floating around that "prisons designated for women are these super trauma-informed, healing, restorative, supportive utopias, which is definitely not what they are." Kief puts it bluntly: maximum security is overused, Indigenous women are over-securitized, guards use force and perform routine strip searches, and other indignities occur that make women's institutions punitive, dehumanizing, and degrading places in which to exist.

But the alternative is often much worse.

Aurora was already on feminizing hormone therapy when she was first incarcerated. CSC took her off it and placed her in a men's institution. It was 18 months before CSC allowed Aurora to continue her medical transition.

In her five years of incarceration, Aurora was housed in six different institutions, because guards would disclose her gender identity and the charge for which she was imprisoned to other incarcerated people "and that would cause issues, and people would want to stab me up, rape me, beat me—take your pick." Kief explains that guards routinely discuss intimate details relating to a person's gender identity where other incarcerated people can hear them, exposing trans people experiencing imprisonment to sexual, physical, and psychological violence from incarcerated people and staff.

"I went through a lot of rapes in the bathrooms," Aurora says, "because there's no cameras in the bathrooms." She felt like "a piece of meat [thrown] to wolves."

More than Their Files

It's true that of the openly trans people in federal custody, most are serving lengthy prison sentences. But this is not because trans people are more likely than their cis peers to commit serious criminal offences. Rather, Matychuk explains, it is more likely the case that trans people serving shorter sentences for relatively minor offences simply decline to disclose their true gender identity in order to protect themselves.

"The only people who feel the need to be trans and out in custody," Matychuk says, "are the people who are there for a very long time."

Indeed, as an openly trans or non-binary person in federal custody, all transitioning does is increase the likelihood that you will become the victim of a violent crime behind bars.

I asked CSC whether it is satisfied with the implementation of *Commissioner's Directive 100*. CSC replied that it is "currently undertaking a compliance review ... which will assist in identifying areas for future amendments to the existing policy framework concerning gender diverse offenders."

The people I spoke to say that several things need to change to make federal institutions a safer and more humane place for incarcerated trans people.

Decisions about transition-related care need to be taken out of CSC's hands, Aurora says. "It has to be through a program outside of their reach and their control, in the community where they can't stop the progress from moving forward."

Correctional officers should be required to undergo ongoing training related to gender identity and diversity, Megan says.

And the "overriding health and safety concerns" clause needs to be dropped from CSC policy, Matychuk insists. It's a cover for systemic transphobic discrimination, and allows CSC to treat trans women as men and trans men as women, when neither is the case.

Matychuk hopes to bring a constitutional challenge to *Commissioner's Directive 100*, alleging discrimination on the basis of sex contrary to Section

15 of the *Canadian Charter of Rights and Freedoms*.[10] For that to occur, she needs incarcerated people to come forward and fight for their rights in court.

Incarcerated trans people have plenty of reasons not to do so: the very real risk of reprisal chief among them. But it's a fight worth having, and all incarcerated trans people stand to benefit.

Too many folks think incarcerated trans people deserve the violence and discrimination they receive in prison, Megan reflects. At best, she says, as "inmates, we quite often feel we're invisible behind these fences. [But] I'm more than just my file."

The New Asylums

Of course, gender dysphoria is not the only—or even the most common—psychiatric disorder that incarcerated people report.

CSC published studies of the prevalence of mental illness amongst federally incarcerated men and incarcerated women in 2015 and 2018, respectively. Those remain the most comprehensive look into the psychiatric disorders of persons serving carceral sentences of two years or more.

Of newly incarcerated men, over 70 percent satisfied the criteria for at least one clinical psychiatric diagnosis; 12.4 percent manifested symptoms of either one of the bipolar disorders, one of the psychotic disorders, or major depression.[11] When you exclude alcohol and substance use disorders as well as antisocial personality disorder—far and away the most prevalent conditions—40 percent of newly incarcerated men still qualified as mentally ill.[12]

Of the 246 incarcerated women CSC interviewed for its 2018 study, 52 percent reported having either one of the bipolar disorders, one of the psychotic disorders, or major depression at some point in their life; 17.9 percent currently reported one of these conditions.[13] Fully a third of the women reporting a current major mental illness showed serious impairments of psychosocial functioning.[14]

Compared to their prevalence amongst Canada's general population, psychosis and major depression are two to four times more common amongst incarcerated people.[15] Antisocial personality disorder is ten times more common.[16]

The figures are even starker in Canada's southern neighbor.

The United States is home to somewhere around 16 percent of all incarcerated people worldwide,[17] despite accounting for only about five percent of the world's total population. That translates to an incarceration rate of 531 per 100,000 persons, using 2021 data.[18] By comparison, Canada incarcerates 88 people per 100,000 members of its general population.

According to one authoritative estimate, from 2016, 20 percent of those incarcerated in a jail and 15 percent of those incarcerated in a state prison meet the criteria for a "serious mental illness."[19] That means there are roughly ten times as many people with severe psychiatric conditions in carceral settings as there are in the United States' hospitals.[20] Whereas somewhere between 0.5 percent and 0.8 percent of the general United States population has schizophrenia, somewhere between 2 percent and 6.5 percent of those behind bars have the condition.[21]

In short, the largest psychiatric facilities in Canada and the United States are the countries' prisons.[22] It is a crisis that is unfolding largely outside of the public eye.

How Did We Get Here?

I have been detained by the police once.

Not long after I took my leave of absence from law school, and with psychosis setting in, I started seeing a shadowy man out of the corner of my eye. One day, that man told me to kill myself, and I dutifully tried to comply. Suffice it to say, I was unsuccessful: the rope with which I tried to hang myself broke, I became scared, and I called 911 for help.

The police arrived shortly thereafter and informed me that they were detaining me under the *Mental Health Act*.[23] What this meant in practice is that they would be taking me to a local hospital for evaluation by a doctor, who would, in turn, decide whether or not to commit me.

By the time the emergency room physician got around to seeing me, however, I was lucid again. And, so, he sent me home.

I have since benefited from the care of a very strong outpatient mental health team, and I have not experienced police intervention in my psychotic episodes again. Many people are not so fortunate.

When mental health crises trigger a state response, it is almost always a police response. It is the end result of decades of deinstitutionalization.

By deinstitutionalization, I mean the removal of brick-and-mortar supports for the seriously mentally ill.

It includes the closure of inpatient psychiatric beds. In 1955 in the United States, "there were 339 occupied state psychiatric beds per 100,000" people; in 1998, "there were 21 occupied state psychiatric beds per 100,000" people.[24] The overall decline of the United States' inpatient psychiatric population in those years was about 90 percent.[25] In 1965, Canada's provincially run hospitals were home to 69,128 inpatient psychiatric beds; by 1981, that figure had dropped 70 percent to 20,301.[26]

The motivating vision behind deinstitutionalization was that—through a combination of new psychopharmaceuticals, like the antipsychotic Thorazine; and strong investment in outpatient mental healthcare—the seriously mentally ill could receive treatment in our communities. But that vision has not come to fruition.

That is because the story of deinstitutionalization in the latter half of the twentieth century is also the story of progressive cutbacks in state (in the United States), provincial (in Canada), and federal (in both) spending on mental healthcare.

In the United States, support for outpatient psychiatric care peaked in the 1960s with the passage of the *Community Mental Health Centers Act* in 1963; and the inauguration of Medicaid in 1965, which provided federal funds for mental healthcare outside inpatient psychiatric settings.[27] The idea was to use federal funds to construct and staff community mental health centers that would, in turn, provide a combination of inpatient, outpatient, and emergency care to the mentally ill. Few actually provided the coordinated care they were mandated to. Twelve years after they were conceived, in 1975, only 675 funded community mental health centers were in operation; 800 communities remained unserved.[28]

Under President Ronald Reagan's *Omnibus Budget Reconciliation Act*, passed in 1981, control of mental healthcare spending was transferred to the states and federal funding reduced by 25 percent. 25 years later, in 2006, the states spent less than 12 percent of the 8 billion USD they had invested in mental healthcare in 1955.[29] During the Great Recession, funding fell further, with states cutting 4.5 billion USD from their financial support for the mentally ill.[30]

In other words, as legal scholar Corrina Lain put it, in the United States deinstitutionalization saw "hundreds of thousands of severely mentally ill people ... discharged from state hospitals with no support structure in place for their care in the community setting."[31]

Something similar played out to the north. There, the withdrawal of government funds from inpatient psychiatric hospitals has not resulted in parallel investments in outpatient care. In British Columbia in 1994-1995, for example, the province's psychiatric units received 424 million CAD in government funding; in 1998-1999, they received 234 million CAD, approximately half as much. Over those same years, funding for outpatient psychiatric services likewise dropped, from 208 million CAD in 1994-1995 to 200 million CAD in 1998-1999.[32]

I want to be very clear here. The problem with deinstitutionalization is not that it emptied the asylums—those were carceral spaces in their own right; and they contributed in no small measure to the afflictions of those they housed, including by aggravating such symptoms as psychosis. The problem is that there was no concomitant investment in outpatient mental healthcare to pick up the slack that the asylums left behind. The prison system has, instead, been left to fill in the gaps.

Deinstitutionalization contributed about four to seven percent of the growth in the United States' carceral population in the last decades of the twentieth century.[33] Thus it is not quite accurate to say that mass incarceration represents the re-institutionalization of the mentally ill. Something else is afoot.

In the United States during the heyday of institutionalization (which peaked in 1955), "state-hospital patients were largely white and middle-aged or older, and divided roughly evenly between men and women; today's incarcerated population is largely young, male, and *not* white."[34] In other words, there was no straightforward translation, post-deinstitutionalization, of the population formerly in psychiatric institutions to the population currently in carceral ones.

It is rather the case that mass incarceration represents the institutionalization of a great many people who would never have been committed to long-term, inpatient psychiatric intervention in the first place. Canada and, to an even greater extent, the United States have criminalized mental illness.

It is all part of a larger politics of death.

The Necropolitics of the Carceral State

These days, it can feel like everyone is mentally ill. At the very least, that mental illness is something everyone talks about. Whether it's on television, on social media, or in public service campaigns, there is a general societal trend underway towards the destigmatization of mental illness and mental healthcare.

But the rising tide of destigmatization has not lifted all boats. There is still a hierarchy of mental illnesses in the public consciousness, and serious mental illnesses like schizophrenia are near the bottom of it.[35]

This is a manufactured result.

One study, which analyzed "newspaper coverage of mental illness in the UK" for the period 1992 to 2008, found a general reduction in negative portrayals of mental illness over the study period; but noted that while coverage of depression improved, it remained "largely negative for schizophrenia."[36] A common television trope depicts schizophrenia as a magical or otherworldly experience, effectively pushing people with the disorder beyond the pale of human understanding.[37] And, of course, there is the media's all too frequent association of psychosis with violence.

As commentator K.J. Aiello observes, the destigmatization of (certain) mental illnesses has been driven by corporate entities:[38] like the telecommunications giant Bell, with its popular Bell Let's Talk campaign encouraging people to discuss their mental health challenges with one another. That means corporate entities have been able to dictate which mental illnesses will benefit from destigmatization and which will be left out. In practical terms, the people who "get" to be mentally ill are those who can choose not to be—by continuing to show up for work, chiefly. The people with debilitating mental illnesses, the people with incomprehensible mental illnesses, the people with terrifying mental illnesses—those people do not get to be mentally ill. They are something else, something worse.

And very often, what they are is "criminals."

There is a divide within Canadian and American society between the lives that matter and the lives that do not. And if we're going to appreciate the nature of this divide, I need to introduce a technical term to describe it: "necropolitics."

The term was first theorized by Achille Mbembe as a decolonical critique of the work of French philosopher Michel Foucault.[39] Necropolitical analysis accepts Foucault's observation that modern states are heavily invested in keeping people alive: whether it is through investment in healthcare infrastructure, roads, and sewers; in providing clean drinking water; or in implementing things like occupational health and safety standards—the modern state does not so much *let* people live as it does *make* people live. But, of course, this is only true in certain parts of the country. For not every individual or every group of people benefits from these life-giving interventions. Some people warrant greater investment than others; some warrant no investment at all. And sovereign power, on this necropolitical analysis, is nothing other than the power to define, specifically, "to define who matters and who does not, who is *disposable* and who is not."[33]

Necropolitics operates spatially and at the level of populations. In Mbembe's terms, the weapons necropower wields "are deployed in the interest of maximum destruction of persons and the creation of *death-worlds*, new and unique forms of social existence in which vast populations are subjected to conditions of life conferring upon them the status of *living dead*."[40] The persons subjected to these weapons are alive yet dead, inhabiting a liminal space in which they merely survive, beyond and without the sustaining power of the state. And the weapons in question take the form, often as not, of withdrawals of state services: a *lack* of healthcare for certain populations, a *lack* of labour rights, a *lack* of security.

Prisons are tools of necropolitical governance. People go there to die. And they go there to die slowly, through unrelenting exposure to violence and scarcity.

Nowhere are the necropolitical dimensions of carceral life more evident than in the prison system's use of isolation tactics: housing people alone in minuscule rooms for 20 to 24 hours each day.

In Canadian penitentiaries, solitary confinement occurs through what are called "structured intervention units" (or "SIU," for short).

These were introduced in 2019 as an alternative to the previous solitary confinement regime, which placed incarcerated people in "administrative segregation." The idea was that stays in SIUs would be rare, short, and less severe than periods of administrative segregation.[41] In fact, two years after the SIUs were established, something like 8.4 percent of all people housed in federal institutions had been placed in one at some point during their incarceration.[36] Nearly half of those held in an SIU in August 2021, when the government studied the units' rollout, were Indigenous.[42] Ten percent received less than four hours of time outside their cells each day. And "of those identified as having various mental health issues and getting worse, 74.6% have been in SIUs for over a month."[43]

Solitary confinement is an exercise, by the state, of what Jasbir Puar calls its "right to maim:"[44] that is to say, of the state's power to debilitate bodies. The experience of solitary confinement can trigger a range of psychiatric symptoms, many of them signs of psychosis.[45] One scholar has even identified a specific psychiatric condition that afflicts those who spend time in penal isolation units. The condition's characteristic features include an inability to tolerate everyday sensory stimuli, such as the sound of a faucet; hallucinations; panic attacks; difficulties with concentration and memory; "intrusive obsessional thoughts;" and paranoia.[46]

Experiencing isolation behind bars breaks minds. It also breaks bodies.

Because solitary confinement is also an exercise, by the state, of the more basic right to kill. One study, from 2019, found that people who endured any length of solitary confinement are 24 percent more likely to die within a year of being released from a carceral setting as their peers who did not. And they are 74 percent more likely to die by suicide.[47]

The point is this: The Canadian and American states assign guilt to certain disabled (and, too often, racialized) populations and then use the apparatus of the criminal justice system to destroy those populations through incarceration. Whether a person is trans in prison or schizophrenic in prison, they are guilty *by virtue of their mental illness* and the state can do what it wants with them. And what the state wants is to destroy them—slowly.

But lest this seem to be about people to the exclusion of God: Something awfully similar happens when Christians label something or someone as *sinful*.

Seven

THE SERPENT'S BITE

IN GENESIS, THE SERPENT tempts Eve with the knowledge of good and evil.

"You are not going to die" if you eat of Eden's forbidden tree, the serpent tells her; "but God knows that as soon as you eat of it your eyes will be open and you will be like divine beings who know good and bad" (Genesis 3:4b-5 JPS).

Of course, we all know that Eve gave in to the serpent's temptation; ate of the forbidden tree; and induced Adam to do the same. This, Christian theology classically teaches, was the original sin: the Fall that subjected everyone who came after to divine judgment.

But why? What was so bad about what Adam and Eve did?

To answer that, we need to look, not in Genesis, but in the Letter to the Romans.

"Sin entered the world through one man, and death through sin," Paul writes there with reference to Adam's actions; "and in this way death came to all people, because all sinned" (Romans 5:12 NIV). The idea is that, somehow, everyone is implicated in Adam's original disobedience of the divine decree not to eat from the Tree of the Knowledge of Good and Evil.

Now, originally, in the years immediately after Paul wrote these words, the idea of an Edenic Fall was a way of doing what theologians call "theodicy," that is, squaring the presence of evil in the world with the existence of a good God. As theologian Ian McFarland puts it, "identifying the ultimate source of evil in the world with an act of creaturely transgression served as a means of defending the Creator against the charges of wickedness or incompetence."[1]

In other words: If people sin, then people—not God—bring evil into the world.

But for Paul, original sin was less a way of defending God's goodness and more a way of explaining God's grace. "The judgment followed one sin and brought condemnation," Paul writes in Romans 5:15 (NIV), "but the gift followed many trespasses and brought justification." There is a simple but powerful idea at work here: If everyone is ensnared in sin, then everyone benefits (or, at least, stands to benefit) from sin's defeat in Christ. "For if," Paul thus goes on to say, "by the trespass of the one man, death reigned through that one man, how much more will those who receive God's abundant provision of grace and of the gift of righteousness reign in life through the one man, Jesus Christ!" (Romans 5:17 NIV) Sin "matters," for Paul, because it makes salvation both necessary and desirable.

The late fourth-century and early fifth-century saint Augustine made a similar move, and in so doing set the stage for Western Christian thinking on sin in the fifteen centuries that have followed his death. Reading the opening chapters of Genesis as a literal depiction of humanity's historical existence in Edenic Paradise, Augustine insisted that Adam's Fall made every human guilty before God.[2] And it did so, in part, because contained within that first sin was every type of sin that humans have subsequently committed.

> For there is pride in it, since man preferred to be under his own rule rather than the rule of God; and sacrilege too, for man did not acknowledge God; and murder, since he cast himself down to death; and spiritual fornication, for the integrity of the human mind was corrupted by the seduction of the serpent; and theft, since the forbidden fruit was snatched; and avarice, since he hungered for more than should have sufficed for him--and whatever other sins that could be discovered in the diligent analysis of that one sin.[3]

But, in Augustine's mind, all this is just another way of saying that every person stands to benefit from God's gracious redemption of the human race. None are saved unless God wants their salvation.[4] "If the good news is that *Jesus* saves," McFarland writes in summary, "and this news is truly *for all* (Luke 2:10-11; cf. Acts 2:39), then it follows that all human beings without distinction *need* saving. For Augustine the doctrine of original sin is vital because it secures this point."[5]

But what, exactly, does Christ save humanity *from*?

In much of Christian thought, it is not "just" hell or damnation or some abstract notion of condemnation. It is physical and mental impairment, too.

For Augustine, human physical difference is the work of humanity's good Creator, whereas disability is the work of human beings themselves. "For God, the Creator of all, knows where and when each thing ought to be, or to have been created, because He sees the similarities and diversities which can contribute to the beauty of the whole," Augustine thus writes in his magnum opus, *The City of God*. "But he who cannot see the whole is offended by the deformity of the part, because he is blind to that which balances it, and to which it belongs."[6] In other words, God creates difference in its beauty; human beings, however, discriminate against difference.

Thus far Augustine's views are consistent with the social model of disability I outlined earlier. But look more closely, and his views start to differ.

That is because, for Augustine, physical impairment has no place in the resurrected life. "The bodies of the saints ... shall rise again free from blemish and deformity," he writes in his handbook of Christian theology, "just as they will be also free from corruption, encumbrance, or handicap. Their facility will be as complete as their felicity."[7] Or as he puts it earlier in the same book, with reference to a case of conjoined twins, "So also in other cases, which, because of some excess or defect or gross deformity, are called monsters: at the resurrection they will be restored to the normal human physiognomy, so that every soul will have its own body and not two bodies joined together, even though they were born this way. Every soul will have, as its own, all that is required to complete a whole human body."[8]

There is an obvious problem here. If human difference is good, why would God do away with it when resurrecting the saints to eternal life? Why, for Augustine and those Christians who follow in his footsteps, does impairment have no place, ultimately, in the climax of the Christian story?

In the passages just quoted, Augustine does not go so far as to explicitly declare impairment or disability products of the Fall. But he implicitly associates bodily difference with sin, death, and fallenness by writing all of these things out of the resurrected life. Impairment, for him, is no more the future of the Christian redeemed than death or damnation.

And therein lies the issue.

"As critics of utopian thinking have long argued," disability theorist Alison Kafer reminds us, "the futures we imagine reveal the biases of the present."[9] And in the futures a great many Christians imagine for themselves, there is neither sin nor disability nor impairment. In their view, I will not be trans or schizophrenic at the resurrection; God will "heal" me of these conditions.

Is that really good news?

Thanks to Paul and Augustine, it is almost impossible to talk about fallenness without talking about redemption. Western Christianity centers the "problem of sin" so that it might offer a curative prescription. We are, it teaches, all of us sinners in need of a savior.

Christianity, obsessed with the redemption of the human race, promulgates what Kafer calls "curative time:" "an understanding of disability that not only *expects* and *assumes* intervention but also cannot imagine or comprehend anything other than intervention."[10] Kafer has medical interventions in view here, but she might as well be referring to Divine ones. And the problem with curative time is not that disabled people cannot or should not desire cures for our impairments. It is that curative time "casts disabled people (as) out of time, or as obstacles to the arc of progress."[11] Disabled people must, on this framing, be moving towards a cure in order to inhabit lives worth living.

But what if disabled lives were already good in themselves? What if disabled bodies and minds *could* be fixed but *need* not be fixed? What if humanity were not fundamentally broken?

What if the problem of sin were no problem at all?

No Redemption

Canada's *Criminal Code* sets out the crimes, punishments, and procedures of Canadian criminal law.[12] And, until the early 2010s, it included something popularly known as the "faint hope clause."[13]

Nestled deep in the provisions having to do with "imprisonment for life," the clause allowed "lifers" to apply for early parole after serving 15 years in prison. The idea behind it was to encourage people sentenced to a life in jail to work to rehabilitate themselves while behind bars.[14] It was rarely used: One study, conducted just before the provision was repealed, found that less than 20 percent of convicted murderers who were eligible for early parole under the faint hope clause were actually successful in obtaining parole.[15]

In 2011, Canada's then-Conservative government abolished the faint hope clause—ostensibly as a way of getting tougher on violent crime, but also under the guise of saving murder victims' families the trauma of attending frequent parole hearings.[16]

Now, on paper at least, criminal sentencing serves a variety of purposes: it's meant to deter people from committing crimes in the future; to denounce criminal behaviour; and to provide for the rehabilitation of those who have already committed criminal acts.[17] With the repeal of the faint hope clause, however, the last of these goals has fallen by the wayside for those who commit the most serious violent crimes. Punishment has taken its place as the overriding goal.

So, too, in Christian thought, where death follows sin. And not only that. The Genesis story tells us that, when Adam and Eve ate of the forbidden tree, God laid curses on them and their descendants. To Eve, God says that "I will make most severe your pangs in childbearing; in pain shall you bear children.

Yet your urge shall be for your husband, and he shall rule over you" (Genesis 3:16 JPS). And to Adam, God says that,

> Because you did as your wife said and ate of the tree about which I commanded you, "You shall not eat of it," Cursed be the ground because of you; by toil shall you eat of it all the days of your life: Thorns and thistles shall it sprout for you. But your food shall be the grasses of the field; by the sweat of your brow shall you get bread to eat, until you return to the ground—for from it you were taken. For dust you are, and to dust you shall return. (Genesis 3:17-19 JPS)

The implied logic of the Edenic Fall, as told in Genesis and interpreted in the light of Augustine and Paul, is that because Adam and Eve violated the Divine law not to eat from the Tree of the Knowledge of Good and Evil, they warranted a divinely imposed sentence. The problem, however, is that the sentence in question far outpaces the nature of the crime, particularly if we assume that it also includes an eternity in hell. God put Adam and Eve in a situation in which obedience meant a continuation of the *status quo*, and disobedience meant not only they but also their progeny would be subject to horrors the likes of which the world had never witnessed and which Adam and Eve would thus not have been able even to imagine.[18] If the theological myth of Eden tells us anything, in other words, it is that God's capacity for retribution is nearly infinite—and lacks anything like the quality of mercy.

This is a problem in its own right, of course, for it is an indictment of the supposedly loving God. But the more immediate problem, for those of us still living on this side of the final judgment, is that Christians too often take it upon themselves to enact divine judgment right now.[19] That looks like everything from denouncing and excluding those whose sins place them beyond the possibility of inclusion in the church catholic; to abusing and even murdering those who, by virtue of who they are (e.g., Indigenous, Black, disabled, women), stand before both God and the Christian condemned.[20] The implied logic is that because some of us are so enmeshed in sin that there is no hope for us in the afterlife, Christians can do what they like with our selves and our bodies in this life.

Now, there is no future for either death or the Edenic curses in Christian thought. "For as in Adam all die," Paul writes in his first letter to the Corinthian church, "so in Christ all will be made alive. But each in turn: Christ, the firstfruits; then, when he comes, those who belong to him" (1 Corinthians 15:22-23 NIV). This penultimate resurrection of the Christian believers will precipitate the end of all things, when Christ hands over all authority to God after he vanquishes his enemies. And "the last enemy to be destroyed is death" (1 Corinthians 15:26 NIV). What God lacks in mercy in Eden, God makes up for in Christ. For it is Christ who overcomes sin and death and thereby brings salvation to the world.

But, in the end, this is God and Christians purporting to solve a problem of God's own making. For it was God who both created humanity to be radically vulnerable to the consequences of original sin *and* imposed those very consequences on us. A life of suffering and disability culminating in death and judgment is the sentence God deems fit for the crime of disobeying the original Divine decree. The "justice" of God is the "justice" of infinite retribution.

And it ought to terrify, just as the possibility of infinite incarceration ought to terrify.

Lucy's Story

Lucy Blacklume is, by all accounts, a dangerous offender.[21]

Since 2008, she has been convicted of, among other things, sexual assault, attempted sexual assault with a weapon, assault causing bodily harm, and most recently in 2019, completed sexual assault with a weapon. She also suffers, most likely, from Fetal Alcohol Spectrum Disorder, "functions cognitively at the level of a 9- or 10-year-old child," lacks the ability to exercise self-control or appreciate the consequences of her actions, and suffers from a range of personality disorders.

And in 2021, the Alberta Court of Appeal sentenced her to what will, in all likelihood, be a life sentence.

The sentence is controversial.

Two years prior, a provincial court judge found that it would constitute cruel and unusual punishment to lock Lucy, an Indigenous woman, away for life.[22] "There is no secure hospital setting available" for a life sentence, the judge concluded. Moreover, "there is limited, if any, availability of music, pet, [or] play therapy" in correctional centers. Lucy would not receive the round-the-clock monitoring necessary to keep her from acting on her suicidal ideation. And, being "biologically male," Lucy would likely be housed in a men's prison despite identifying as female.

The Court of Appeal disagreed. Lucy's many struggles are no different from those of other dangerous offenders, and her transgender identity is irrelevant for sentencing. What matters, in deciding what to do with her, is not what's best for Lucy or even other inmates, but rather what's necessary to ensure public safety. In this case, "the Crown has adduced ample proof that a sentence [of indeterminate and likely lifetime length] is required to provide adequate protection of the public against Ms Blackplume's committing a serious personal injury offence."

But you know what? If we were serious about public safety, Lucy would not have wound up in prison at all.

———

Lucy's sentence is controversial in another respect.

As I have already pointed out, Correctional Service Canada policy since 2022 has been to incarcerate people according to their gender identity, provided that is their preference.[23] And it has been to do so irrespective of "their anatomy (sex) or gender on their identification documents, unless there are overriding health or safety concerns which cannot be resolved."[24] Apparently, Lucy didn't express a desire to be housed in a women's prison; hence she found herself bound for a men's facility, instead.

That will be good news for certain activists. For in Canada, as in other jurisdictions like California with similar policies regarding the placement of transgender offenders,[25] housing incarcerated trans women in women's prisons has drawn strong opposition from "trans-exclusionary radical feminists"—or, as they are more commonly known, "TERFs."

In June 2021, a group of criminalized women sent an open letter to the Canadian Association of Elizabeth Fry Societies (a prison abolitionist organization that combats the criminalization and social exclusion of women and gender-diverse people) calling on the organization to support a blanket ban on what the authors characterized (in my view, transphobically) as "male transfers to women's prisons."[26] Indeed, the authors of that letter asserted, "every one of us knows a woman who has either been harassed, sexually harassed, assaulted, or sexually assaulted by a male transfer to a women's prison"[27]—a claim that played on the anti-trans trope of the predatory trans woman.[28] The inclusion of trans women inmates in any women's "prison that is already damaging and oppressive is triggering for us."[29]

Canadian Women's Sex-Based Rights ("CAWSBAR"), Canada's most active TERF organization,[30] has likewise made keeping trans women out of women's prisons one of its key issues. Many women inmates have a history of male victimization, CAWSBAR argues on its website. Consequently, "forcing [those inmates] to be imprisoned with violent male [*sic*] predators constitutes cruel and unusual punishment,"[31] presumably because their trans women co-inmates have an inherent predisposition towards re-victimizing them. Together with radical feminist organization We the Females, CAWSBAR has staged a number of protests at prisons across Canada against CSC's gender self-identification policy.[32]

I do not deny the possibility of an incarcerated trans woman committing sexual violence in a women's prison: *Any incarcerated person* could do so, regardless of their gender identity. But I admit to being perplexed by the TERF obsession with removing trans women from women's prisons, for a simple reason: In what world is it "radical" to argue for a different distribution of prisoners amongst carceral institutions, rather than for the abolition of those institutions themselves?

The one TERFs inhabit, apparently.

I should think, instead, that a truly radical feminist politics would be an abolitionist one.

Against the Carceral State

Abolition is "an overarching movement to dismantle the carceral system and reimagine what public safety could look like by addressing the root cause of crime."[33] It is anti-prison, anti-police, anti-punishment; and pro-accountability, pro-community change, and pro-healing.

The feminist case against prisons is one that recognizes that the criminal justice system is itself a vector of colonial and patriarchal violence.

I have already detailed the overincarceration of the mentally ill. But consider, too, the over-incarceration of Indigenous women. Indigenous women account for four percent of Canada's female population,[34] but more than half of all women in federal carceral institutions.[35] These figures are all the more striking given that, while Canada's reported crime rates have nearly halved since 1990,[36] "admissions to women's federal correctional facilities more than tripled" over the same period.[37] Small wonder that Canada's prisons have come to be associated with the historical genocide of Canada's Indigenous peoples.

Within prisons themselves, guards commit violence against inmates along disproportionately racial lines. The 2020-2021 report of the Office of the Correctional Investigator found that "BIPOC women account[] for more than two-thirds of all women involved in uses of force," in particular, Indigenous women make up 60 percent of all victims of use-of-force incidents.[38] The Office also found that, overall, women's prisons continue to suffer from "inadequate infrastructure, over-securitization, lack of programming and services, poor community reintegration practices," and a governing "frame-work that puts security and control at the forefront."[39]

Women's penitentiaries, in short, are sites of state violence against racially marginalized women. Plain and simple.

All of this would be an indictment of Canada's criminal justice system even if the country's current approach to incarceration could be shown to reduce and prevent crime, especially violent crime.

The problem? *It can't.*

Ignore for a moment the fact that most crimes are property offences or victimless "quality of life" offenses that target unhoused people in particu-lar for things like loitering.[40] Even if we focus only on violent crimes, the research shows that incarceration does little to promote public safety. The United States imprisons more people per capita than any other country in the world.[41] Yet one recent study found that "sentencing someone to prison [for a violent crime] had no effect on their chances of being convicted of a violent crime within five years of being released from prison,"[42] indicating that prison does nothing to rehabilitate violent offenders or prevent future offenses. Indeed, the United States' sky-high incarceration rate has decreased neither crime rates in general nor general violence more particularly.[43]

If prisons kept us safe, Canada's southern neighbor would be the safest country in the world. But they don't. Indeed, as one Australian activist put it back in 2009, "if all our organizations had the extended failure rate that the prison system has, we would [all] be de-funded and out of work."[44]

What prisons *do* is isolate incarcerated people from the support networks and community resources that can actually make a difference in preventing crime, rehabilitating offenders, and helping victims.

Abolishing them, not reforming them, needs to be the priority for every feminist who is serious about protecting women.

And what is hell, as traditionally conceptualized, but the ultimate prison: A place of eternal suffering and torment for those beyond the reach of the redemption that Christianity offers its adherents? What is hell but an exten-sion, into perpetuity, of the debility, the cursedness, and the pain that God imposed on humanity at Adam's fall? What is the hell to which Christians condemn non-believers but an evil that must be destroyed?

Original Fears

I came honestly to the idea that I was inherently guilty before God.

Growing up in the conservative evangelicalism of the Christian and Missionary Alliance in Canada, I was exposed from a young age to the inevitability of damnation for those who reject Christ's loving embrace. "The destiny of the impenitent and unbelieving is existence forever in conscious torment," the denomination's statement of faith declares, "but that of the believer is everlasting joy and bliss."[45] And I knew which side of that equation I wanted to be on.

I did everything right. I accepted Jesus as my personal lord and savior. I attended church on Sundays; youth group on Wednesdays; small group on Fridays; and, whenever I could, Christian summer camps, weekend retreats, and concerts. Whenever I had the opportunity—and there were *always* opportunities—I recommitted myself and my life to Jesus. And it was never, ever enough.

Here's the dirty little secret of evangelical Protestantism in North America: no matter how much it might stress the idea of salvation by faith alone, in practice it demands adherents *do* quite a lot to secure their eternal futures. Because no matter how many times I claimed Jesus as my own, there was always a lurking suspicion in the back of my mind that I had not done it "properly;" that I might get to the End of All Things and hear those haunting words of Jesus, recorded in Matthew's Gospel: "I never knew you. Away from me, you evildoers!" (Matthew 7:23 NIV) So I kept praying, hoping that one of my prayers might eventually be enough to ensure I would join Jesus in that heavenly paradise.

It seems almost inevitable, in hindsight, that my childhood fear of eternal damnation would carry over into my psychosis.

I was 25 when I started hearing the devil's voice and feeling his presence wherever I went. He threatened me, followed me, commanded me to hurt myself. He put images into my head of the torture, violence, and suffering that awaited me in hell. I *knew* I was damned, as clearly as I knew the sky was blue. And there was nothing I could do about it, because the devil had marked me as his own.

I was a sinner in need of a savior. But my savior had abandoned me.

Whether it is the justice of death and hell or that of mass incarceration, retribution offers no reassurances. It can inspire fear, but no more. Whether it is applied to "sinners" or to "criminals," retributive justice matches evil with evil, death with death. It says that some people are so beyond redemption they are fit only for the slow destruction that is indefinite damnation and the whittling away of their person that incarceration effects.[46]

But if we take the story of Eden seriously, then this is the very essence of sin: To be able, as creatures, to bring our moral intuitions to bear on the actions of our Creator. God acknowledges as much. "The man has become like one of us," God admits in Genesis 3:22 (JPS), "knowing good and bad." And that alone warrants a death sentence, lest Adam, Eve, and their progeny "stretch out [their] hand and take also from the tree of life, and live forever!" (Genesis 3:22 JPS)

In other words, our fallenness puts we humans in the position of being able to judge Godself. To look upon what God does and to discern the good and the bad in it. To critique God, talking back when God gives us a command. To protest.

And what's so evil about that?

Theology is nothing other than discourse about the Divine. It is "God talk." It can take formal shape, like this book; but it can also take the shape of our everyday intuitions and reflections on who God is and what God does. Either way, the fact that we do theology as sinners gives our theologizing its critical edge. I wouldn't give it up even if I had the choice, even if it meant never experiencing another psychotic episode again, even if it meant living forever. For our fallenness is immensely potent. It gives us our voice.

The Material Realities of Rape Culture

To be a transgender woman in this age of rising anti-trans hate is to be at once supremely powerful and supremely vulnerable.

Powerful, because in the eyes of our enemies we erase women,[47] destroy women's spaces,[48] and subject children to the sexual violence of "grooming" simply by existing.[49] Vulnerable, because our supposed omnipotence is no protection against a seemingly unyielding wave of bills meant to legislate us out of existence, the torrent of harassment we experience on and offline, or the record-high levels of fatal violence committed against members of our community.[50]

Depending on where you stand on the question of whether trans people should exist within the body politic, feminism is either to thank or to blame for this state of affairs. Either way, though, feminism is responsible.

TERFs have been likening male-to-female gender transition to sexual violence at least since radical feminist Janice Raymond published *The Transsexual Empire* in 1980.[51] There, she wrote: "All transsexuals [*sic*] rape women's bodies by reducing the real female form to an artifact, appropriating this body for themselves."

Whether Raymond intended this assertion to be metaphorical is perhaps a matter of interpretation. Whether today's trans-exclusionary feminists intend the assertion literally is not.

The "Cotton Ceiling = Rape" claims UK-based "lesbian feminist activist group" Get the L Out, referring to the way trans lesbians supposedly pressure their cisgender counterparts into sex in order to affirm their (the trans women's) identity as women. This is the same group that forced its way into the 2018 London Pride march to distribute pamphlets claiming trans women are rapists.

In the United States, the Women's Liberation Front (WoLF) wrongly insists that including trans women in women's spaces makes rape possible where it wasn't, "because a man's biology [i.e., his having a penis] gives him the ability to rape a woman, while her biology [i.e., her lack of a penis] makes her incapable of raping him."[52] Ignoring the fact that cis women can and do sexually assault people of all genders, in WoLF's view the mere possibility of rape means cis women need sex-segregated spaces for their own protection—even if no trans woman has ever actually assaulted a cis woman in a women's space. As they themselves say, WoLF doesn't "need it to be true that there are any cases of rape in [e.g.,] a woman's prison to make an argument against a male [*sic*] being transferred to a women's prison."[53]

The bottom line: trans women are a threat, and if (cis) women are to be safe, trans women must be kept far away from cis women's spaces.

If this sounds familiar, it's because in the culture war over trans women's rights this argument has become a rallying cry for feminists and non-feminists alike. "Male" trans women are the specter haunting cis women everywhere from bathrooms to sports, and the only way to save those cis women is to save sex-segregated women's spaces.

TERF rhetoric has gone mainstream.

This puts feminism's future as a political movement capable of materially advancing women's interests in serious doubt.

Trans-exclusionary feminism substitutes anxieties about the *potential* threat that trans women pose to cis women's safety for *actual concern* about protecting women from sexual violence.

The possibility of trans women committing rape is enough by itself to exclude them, as a class, from women's spaces altogether. And that possibility will always be there because trans women either have or (in the case of those who have had a vaginoplasty operation) had a penis—the ultimate weapon of patriarchal violence.

Personally, I'd prefer it if the penis were a shield.

As I and other trans women survivors of sexual violence know, however, our genitalia at birth are anything but.

Roughly half of all trans people experience sexual assault during their lifetime,[54] and trans people are four times more likely to be victims of violent crimes than cisgender people.[55]

Moreover, whether the sexual assaults occur in elementary schools, home-less shelters, or prisons, the victims tend to be trans women rather than trans men.[56]

This data confirms what trans social critics have been arguing for years: in a patriarchal society that affords men a higher place within the gender caste structure, those "men" who choose to become women and move "down" the gender hierarchy are dealt with especially harshly.

There's nothing symbolic, metaphorical, or potential about the sexual violence we trans women suffer.

It's physical. Material. A story of patriarchal dominance that's written on the bodies of survivors with each thrust of those who attack us.

Ain't I A Survivor, Too?

As a movement, feminism is premised on two ideas. First, that women are more alike than different because we all to some degree experience gendered oppression. Second, that the only way to finally banish this oppression is for the oppressed to unite as a political class and campaign for our liberation.

From its inception, feminism has struggled with the question of whom to include in this class, long framed as the question of whom to include in the category "women." White feminists have historically answered this question in a way that excludes women of color; upper-class and upwardly mobile middle-class feminists have historically answered it in a way that excludes women of the working class.

Feminism's great shame is that the women most in need of gender-based rights and protections have been asking, as African American abolition-ist and women's rights advocate Sojourner Truth did in 1851, "Ain't I a woman?"—and feminists have been replying, "No."

That is an important question, to be sure. But I don't think it's the most important one, not in the current political moment anyway.

To see why, we need to look beyond philosophical debates about the nature of womanhood and focus, instead, on material realities.

Rape is the archetypal expression of gendered oppression. It is the most potent, violent, and dehumanizing way by which men assert their superiority over women and those they read as women (trans men, for instance).

That's why, no matter who feminists count as women, rape is the monster that above all others they set out to slay.

The problem with trans-exclusionary feminism is that it not only excludes from the feminist coalition the very people most in need of feminist political victories; but by campaigning to keep those same people in men's spaces, it actively renders them more vulnerable to the very violence feminism most opposes.

In other words, trans-exclusionary feminism is anti-feminist because it actually promotes gendered sexual violence under the guise of protecting women.

Philosophical questions about whether trans women are really women or trans men are really men are a luxury that goes out the window when a person is being forced to have sex without their consent.

That's why the foundational question for feminist organizing has to be something more firmly grounded in the material realities of gendered existence. That's why feminists should never have allowed ourselves to become bogged down in the question of whether trans women are also women. That's why feminism must rid itself of its trans-exclusionary wing.

Because if feminism is truly a movement against patriarchal violence, those subjected to the worst of that violence are feminism's heart and soul.

The foundational question for feminist organizing should not be whether trans women are "woman-enough" for the feminist movement. We are, but that only matters so much.

The foundational question is this: Are we not survivors, too?

We are—in horrifying numbers.

Which is why, if feminism is to succeed in dismantling the patriarchy, it must be more than just trans-inclusive: it must actively and unabashedly fight for trans liberation.

Wrong Questions, Wrong Answers

Radical feminists, instead, spend their time and activist energy asking which prison someone like Lucy Blackplume should spend her life in. That's the wrong question. And it's borne of a fundamental misapprehension of what keeps women safe.

Every crime is an indictment of the society that created the conditions for it to happen in the first place. It represents a failure on the whole of society to combat rape culture and misogyny; and to provide the mental health, addictions support, affordable housing, and other community-level interventions that actually prevent crimes from occurring. Every sin is an indictment, too: but of God. For every sin represents a failure on the part of the Divine to create a more humane world.

For these reasons, abolitionist justice like abolitionist theology responds to violent acts by calling for both the individual and the societal changes that are necessary to ensure that neither a particular person nor the world at large reoffends.

So what do we do with someone like Lucy Blackplume?

Disinvest in the structures that perpetuate violence against women like her; and invest, instead, in the structures that help both victims and offenders.

Lucy's case is a miscarriage of justice not because she probably wound up in a men's prison. It is a miscarriage of justice because she wound up in prison at all and was denied the care she needs to overcome her many struggles. It is a miscarriage of justice because Lucy's case represents a failure to include her in the body politic—as an Indigenous woman, as a disabled woman, as a woman. It is a miscarriage of justice because she'll be further pushed to the margins of society, but nothing about her society—*our* society—will change in response. Unless, that is, we fight for change to occur.

The TERFs are right: trans women like Lucy shouldn't be housed in women's prisons. But that's about all the TERFs get right. Because no one should be housed in women's prisons: women's prisons shouldn't exist at all.

Want to get serious about radical feminism? Push for a future without prisons either in this life or the next.

PART FOUR
Evil, Damnation

My dreams have been unusually vivid of late.

I'm on the psychiatric ward at the South Health Campus. Bright rays of sunshine are streaming in through the wide glass windows that line the psychiatrist's office. She's explaining that it will be some time still before I'm able to go home. I'm extremely sick, although with what she does not know. I find this news more comforting than alarming; it's safe here.

I've never been hospitalized on that ward.

I'm back at college. I've just been kicked out of my family home and I need to find new accommodations. There's a flat near the school that I can afford, and I move in. It's quiet; I can ride my bike to class.

I didn't lose my family home until law school.

We're sitting on the edge of the bed in my childhood room. I can make out the subtle notes of your perfume. You put your hand on my knee and lean in. We share a kiss that lasts moments, but feels like a lifetime.

That home was sold more than a decade ago.

———

As I write this, I can only just distinguish my dreams from my memories.

The former feel so real, so believable, that I have a hard time telling myself they're not.

My schizophrenic mind has constructed an elegant explanation for this. My dreams *are* real, but they're taking place in an alternate reality that only I can glimpse. One in which I was hospitalized at the South Health Campus, I did lose my home in undergrad, we were together—and it was beautiful.

This is a delusional explanation, I'm sure; although a significant part of me wants to think otherwise. There's something tranquil about the world I am dreaming up. I want to live there myself.

Sometimes, living with schizophrenia means living inside a waking nightmare. One in which you're tormented by monsters, the devil is trying to drag you to hell, God is cursing you, and the help you receive from others takes the form of condescension and incarceration.

Sometimes, living with schizophrenia means living inside a reverie, more pleasant than fearful.

But it always, in my case, means inhabiting a world in which reality is permeable. One in which angels and demons are breaking free of their domain to vie for attention in mine. One in which fanciful ideas come out of nowhere and immediately command belief. One in which all of this feels as real, as normal, as my morning cup of coffee.

One in which I have to choose what to accept as true, and what to dismiss as mere symptoms of my illness.

I doubt anyone else will agree that my dreams are actually visions. But, truth be told, I've long since stopped caring.

See, here's the thing about my delusions. They come to me as intuitions about the world. And those intuitions have the same force, the same inherent plausibility, the same weight as any of my more "mainstream" beliefs—you know, the kind I feel comfortable sharing at parties. That's what makes my delusions so hard to dismiss, even when they're distressing.

My delusions don't feel like someone else's beliefs, even when they're new. They feel like mine.

I am under near-constant bombardment by these beliefs. Which means I am near-constantly having to choose which to believe.

Sometimes, rarely, the delusions are beautiful. And when they are, is there anything more human than choosing to believe them, simply because they make your reality a better place? Is there anything more human than having this little bit of faith?

Eight

PARANOID READING, PARANOIA

AT ONE POINT IN time, psychoanalysis could reasonably claim the support of much of the psychiatric and psychological professions. But these days, its most devoted supporters are in the field of literary studies. Small wonder, then, that it was in a comparative literature course I took during my first semester at Yale University that I was exposed to the long shadow Sigmund Freud and his followers continue to cast over the literary academy.[1]

Yale's historic Old Campus is a long walk from the School of Divinity, where I was based as a master's student. And as I made my way down Prospect Hill each week, to sit around the expansive wooden table of our seminar room in Linsly-Chittenden Hall, what I was most aware of was not the leaves slowly changing color on the many elm trees in the Elm City—it was the number of police cars that passed me by. In the cheerful town of New Haven in the late 2010s, there were *a lot of them*. And I knew that each one was surveilling me, that soon one would stop me, and that before I knew it I would end up arrested on some trumped up charge.

With the benefit of hindsight, I know now that I was probably experiencing one of my first episodes of psychosis. But at the time, I shared my fears and suspicions with no one.

Why would I? After all, the police were bugging my apartment, eavesdropping on my calls, and monitoring my computer. If they knew I was in on all that, wouldn't they simply kick down my door and call it a day? So I suffered in silence. I went whole weeks without leaving my apartment because I did not want to chance running into a cop on the sidewalk. I memorized the phone numbers of local lawyers who specialized in criminal law, so I knew whom to call when I was detained—as I knew I would be, eventually. I listened at the front door for the sound of approaching feet, ready to flee if necessary.

I watched, and I waited, and nothing ever happened. Until one day, the paranoia lifted. I do not remember when, exactly; it was sometime late in my second semester. But I stopped worrying that the police were after me. And life went on.

———

Paranoia is a much-prized disposition in the field of critical literary theory.

That's the point Eve Kosofsky Sedgwick made in her landmark essay "Paranoid Reading and Reparative Reading, or, You're So Paranoid, You Probably Think This Essay Is About You."[2] But as Sedgwick notes, it's a problem.[3]

For Sedgwick, paranoia is a way of knowing—and it "knows some things well and others poorly."[4] Thus, paranoia as a critical practice is different from paranoia as a symptom of, say, schizophrenia. The former is not delusional, nor is it necessarily wrong about the world;[5] but what it gets right, it only gets right in part.

We will return to Sedgwick's curative prescription later in this book. For now, let us dwell with her diagnosis of the disease.

Paranoid reading is "anticipatory," Sedgwick finds: "because there must be no bad surprises, and because learning of the possibility of a bad surprise would itself constitute a bad surprise, paranoia requires that bad news be always already known."[6] Paranoid reading is "reflexive and mimetic:" the paranoid reader subjects themselves to the very horrors they know, intuitively, are out there, for example by criticizing themselves the way they "know" others will.[7] Paranoid reading is "strongly tautological:" it proves the very things it assumes, over and over and over again, even as it presents each paranoid conclusion as a triumph of critical inquiry.[8] Affectively, paranoid reading is strongly negative and profoundly pessimistic: rather than seek pleasure, it seeks only to forestall pain.[9] Finally, paranoid reading "places its faith in exposure:" it assumes the naïveté of others; and presumes that, if only it can make known the grim "truth" about the world, others will be spurred to action.[10]

And once paranoia takes hold, it is difficult to shake.[11]

Now, paranoia is not intrinsically problematic. Even a paranoid person can have enemies, after all; and is it not some consolation to know who those enemies are?

Paranoia rather becomes problematic when it is one's only way of looking at the world: when you're paranoid all the way down, then you need help. And that's because paranoia warps your ability to trust others.

If everyone is potentially out to get you, no one can be your friend. Which is why to be paranoid is, first and foremost, to be alone. And that is no way to live.

Paranoia—be it the psychotic kind or the kind practiced in comparative literature courses at Yale—is a shield. And when it comes to something like the Bible or the Christian theological tradition, we need the protection paranoid interpretation confers because both have the capacity to hurt us in profound ways. We will have reason, later in this book, to cultivate a more trusting relationship with each of them, to be sure. But it will be because we were first paranoid and subsequently *chose* to let down our guard.

Paranoia has its uses, after all.

"No."

I studied the Bible before I studied theology.

I was 18 years old and unsure of my place in the world. But I had grown up conservative evangelical; going to Bible college made as much sense as grabbing a safety blanket during a thunderstorm. So after I graduated from high school, I enrolled in a degree program in biblical studies. It happened to be offered by the undergraduate institution of my childhood denomination; it happened to be located in my hometown. It felt safe. And I excelled.

But studying the Bible as intensely as I did shook my faith in its certainties.

I had grown up a young earth creationist and a biblical literalist. Academic biblical studies quickly reduced those convictions to shards of broken glass. It was the usual things that did it for me. Learning that the five books of "Moses" are actually multiple literary works edited together over time, and identifiable today as separate texts.[12] Learning how much the Genesis creation narratives have in common with other ancient Near Eastern creation myths. Discovering the total lack of evidence for anything like a historical Exodus from Egypt.

But it was other things, too. I read the Bible more closely than I had ever read it before, and its contents horrified me. I read the story, in Judges 19-21, of the Levite's concubine—raped, abused, and, finally, dismembered—and could not imagine how such a tale could possibly be the Word of God. I saw how God spoke to his people through the prophet Hosea—how God personified his people as an abused woman, and Godself as her abuser—and asked myself if I really believed this to be a faithful depiction of the Divine.

In the end, I said "No."

In the end, I left conservative evangelicalism not because I started believing in evolution or the fact that Moses didn't write the five books attributed to him. I left conservative evangelicalism because I needed to inhabit a space in which it was acceptable to talk back to the God that Scripture reveals. I left conservative evangelicalism because my "No" became the foundation for a new and more generous faith in which I started to say "Yes" to all the things I had been taught to despise: feminism, 2SLGBTQ+ inclusion, love. And I sought that faith in liberal Anglicanism.

Some years later, I was sitting in a psychiatrist's office answering questions about my gender identity as a trans woman. What, the psychiatrist wanted to know, would a much younger me think about how I had turned out? To which I answered: the conservative evangelical culture in which I grew up was so repressive, a younger me wouldn't even be able to imagine the possibilities I eventually grew into. She would need to read the Bible first.

The Social Construction of the Bible

If you have spent any amount of time with different Christian communities, you will know that when different people talk about the Bible, they are talking about different things. There are the obvious differences, of course: Roman Catholics and many Anglicans, among others, have more books in their Bibles than do Protestants, who reject the "Deuterocanon" (books like Tobit and 1 Maccabees) as apocryphal and extra-canonical. But I mean more than this. Ask a liberal Anglican and a conservative evangelical to read Genesis 1, and it will quickly become apparent that they are reading different things: the former a theological myth; the latter a historically and scientifically accurate rendering of the creation of all things.

These differences are substantial. They go to the very question of what the Bible actually is, as an entity in the world. And what they show is that the Bible exists, first and foremost, *in people's minds*. Its meaning is not "out there," in the real world. We cannot reach out and touch it. It is internal to the consciousness of the Bible's readers.

Now, you are probably thinking at this point that I am missing something obvious: the Bible *is* "out there." You can go to the store and buy a copy of it. You can hold it in your hands, turn its pages, and take in its scent. And when someone says something is in the Bible, you can go to the Bible and check whether that person is or is not telling the truth. So what am I even talking about?

I am talking about the social construction of reality.[13] And just so you can understand what I mean, I will need to get technical for a moment.

The world is composed of subjects and objects. "I" am the subject of my consciousness; therefore, I perceive "you"—my reader—and "it"—this book—as "Others." These Others have an independent existence that is external to me. Neither you nor this book ceases to exist when I stop thinking about the same. However, I cannot encounter you or this book or anything else except through my own internal cognitive processes, which are, in turn, shaped by external social forces.

Subjects interact with one another over time, and those interactions have a conditioning effect. I start to "know" certain things about the world because that is what my community knows: for example, that those funny slips of paper we all carry around in our wallet have value and can be exchanged for material goods; that some actions are "right" and others "wrong" or even "criminal;" that some people belong in our community by virtue of the place they were born or the color of their skin, while others do not; that certain ways of inhabiting the world are typical of those assigned male at birth, while others are not. As individuals, we do not choose these socially constructed facts; they are chosen for us by our societies and comprise the "cultural matrix" into which we are socialized over time, sometimes beginning at birth.[14]

All of which is to say that the "stuff" of reality—the objects that extend through space and that we take for granted as "real"—only "matter" insofar as we make sense of them as people. The sixteenth-century essayist Michel de Montaigne was quite right when he wrote, "We need to interpret interpretations more than to interpret things."[15] Humans make the world real by making sense of its contents and living our lives in accordance with the same.

Like money, morals, race and national identity, and gender, texts are socially constructed entities. But that does not mean they do not exist. It just means that they always exist in relation to subjects. The Bible—as an example of one such text—exists to and for *me*, and to and for *you*. Which is just to say: if we are to understand what the Bible *is*, you need to get to know me and I need to get to know you. We need to understand where each of us comes from and what our communities have taught us to believe.

Relationship is the prerequisite to knowledge. Because, if you are a conservative evangelical, for example, Genesis 1 really *is* a litany of scientific facts about the world; while if you are a liberal Anglican, it really isn't. And the really interesting thing is, *why*.

Insight

Schizophrenia disrupts your ability to distinguish the things of this world from the things of your mind. In its most intense form, this disruption manifests as something called *anosognosia*, a lack of personal insight into the fact that one is experiencing a mental illness in the first place.[16] But even when you know you are sick—as I do during all but the darkest of my psychotic episodes, and almost always since I started taking antipsychotics—the voices I hallucinate sound as real as the ones I "actually" hear during my day-to-day life. The scream I heard while writing this chapter was substantial enough that I had to ask my partner if they were okay or if I had just heard them in distress.

It can be just as difficult to distinguish the social constructs that structure our lives from the "really real" objects that populate our world. I might know that gender is a socially constructed entity, say; that does not mean it does not still structure my experience day-to-day. And therein lies the point: insight does not equate to action. I knew at the time that the scream I heard this morning was an auditory hallucination, a trick my mind was playing on me—I don't live in the kind of neighbourhood where shrill notes of distress are particularly common, after all. That does not mean I did not hear it, or respond accordingly. Just as, when I hear footsteps behind me on my walk home from the bus stop, I quicken my pace even though I know there is no one there. The devil is not putting thoughts into my head; he has not marked me as his own or dispatched his demonic legions to drag me down to hell—I still worry about it, even though I know that these are delusions that my mind is feeding me.

One of the problems Sedgwick identifies with the paranoid reading position is that it does not inspire any particular course of action. It assumes, instead, that once it has revealed the grand conspiracy against the paranoid person, that revelation will itself accomplish something. "That a fully initiated listener could still remain indifferent or inimical, or might have no help to offer," Sedgwick writes, "is hardly treated as a possibility."[17] But it is a possibility the actualization of which those of us with clinical paranoia know all too well.

The Illuminati and Me

My paranoia returned about a year-and-a-half after I graduated from Yale. Only, this time, it took the form of the much stranger belief that the mythical Illuminati were watching and scheming against me.

I started keeping a close eye on the number of white cars on my street. The Illuminati drive white cars—I knew this to be true the same way I knew that a blue sky means the sun is out. They were after me. They had been after me from the beginning. The more white cars there were on my street, the more closely I was being surveilled. (White is the most common car color.[18] I was always being watched.)

These convictions persisted even after my condition was otherwise stabilized through high doses of antipsychotic medication. Which is just to say that I have a condition that cannot be cured, that I will always be sick.

I wonder, sometimes, how my adult life might have turned out differently had I not been cursed with recurrent waves of paranoid thinking. To this day, I cannot watch movies that too heavily feature conspiracies or secret organizations, for fear that my addled brain will be unable to distinguish between reality and what I see on the silver screen. I avoid reading the biblical prophets for fear that my schizophrenic mind will again internalize the idea that *I* am a prophet. I walk quickly past the prominent display of occult books at my favorite local bookstore. These days, I am probably as paranoid about potential triggers for my paranoia as I am about the objects of my paranoia itself.

You don't have to convince me that the world is a fundamentally unsafe place. I already know this to be true. But no matter how much I might plead with others, no one else ever seems to know this themselves.

Life without Fear

The Bible has an extraordinary capacity to hurt people. And that is because, for many of us, it is more than just a book like any other. It is the very Word of God. So the issue with it is not just that it is replete with texts that can be used to terrorize women and racialized people;[19] it is that those same texts carry the Divine imprimatur. And we really believe that. We know it to be true. After all, if we didn't, it would no more matter to us what the Bible has to say about women, say, than what the Code of Hammurabi does.

Which is why merely pointing out—as if reciting a litany of horrors—all the ways in which the Bible justifies—or, which is the same, all the ways it can be used to justify—misogyny, racism, transphobia, and so forth does not get people very far. Because even if the Bible *does* justify all those things, as I think it does, we still, as people for whom the Bible is *Scripture*, need to find some way of using this text. We still need to lay claim to it as ours in some way.

Paranoid reading, like clinical paranoia, ends where it starts: in a place of fear. And fear inhibits rather inspires action. When I was most afraid of "them"—be they the police or the Illuminati—my response was to shutter myself in my home. And so, too, if we are afraid of the Bible, our natural response will be not to read it. To throw it and the God it reveals away, like the proverbial baby with the bathwater. And to distance ourselves from those who continue to cling to the Bible as the prime example of Divine revelation. But those are mistakes.

To be paranoid is to be alone—in one's fears and, if one inhabits those fears with too much intensity, in the world itself. And that is no way to live. But we can know that there are things in the world with the capacity to hurt us, even badly, without slipping into paranoia. We can choose not to be afraid of them. We can choose to live with them, instead.

Let's start with the prince of fear himself: the devil.

Nine

BEING DAMNED, BEING TRANS

I.

IN THE BEGINNING, GOD *formed Adam in his own image.*

*"Worship the image of the Lord God, just as the Lord God has commanded,"
Michael instructed the other angels—although God himself had given no such
instruction. But the devil refused.*

*So Michael tried to force the devil to pay obeisance. But still the devil refused.
"Before this man was made," the devil reasoned, "I had already been made.
He ought to worship me." Hearing this, some of the other angels agreed with the
devil and joined him in his refusal to bow.*

*"If you do not worship this man," Michael warned, "the Lord God will grow
angry with you." But this did not faze the devil. "If God grows angry with me,"
he replied, "I will place my seat above the stars of heaven and I will be like the
Most High."*

*This angered God. And in that anger, God expelled the devil and his angelic
allies from heaven. Cast onto the face of the earth, they mourned; for God had
deprived them of their glory, while Adam enjoyed the pleasures of Eden.*

Thus did the devil fall, according to The Life of Adam and Eve.[1]

II.

Transphobia isn't just everywhere. For the most part, it's also really funny.

I suspect that, on some level, just about everybody knows this to be true. But it's one of those basic facts about the world that I, at least, wasn't able to acknowledge until after I'd also come to the realization that I myself am trans.

A transgender woman, to be more precise. This means that, when I was born, a doctor looked between my legs and declared me a boy; and I've been unhappy about that pronouncement ever since. It also means that I experience the particular version of anti-trans hostility known as transmisogyny,[2] a form of bigotry that basically says the only thing worse than being a woman is being a man who *chooses* to be a woman—because no one who's tasted of male privilege could actually *want* to be a member of the inferior sex, amirite?

Those dudes you hear about who get off wearing stockings and dresses? The ones who put on a feminine disguise to prey on women in bathrooms and locker rooms? The shemale traps who lure straight men into having gay sex? Yeah, I'm one of those.

And, truth be told, I have it pretty easy.

That's because I'm white. And, being white, my experience of transmisogynistic bigotry is unlikely to rise above the level of discrimination and sexual harassment. I simply don't have as much reason to fear physical and sexual violence as do trans women of color, who are substantially more likely to be assaulted or murdered or abused by police.[3] If a twentysomething white girl like me dies, it's probably because I've killed myself;[4] indeed, every time I experience discrimination or harassment, the probability that I will engage in self-harm more than doubles.

I am a white trans girl who, for the three years preceding my graduation from seminary, worshiped and (for one of those years) worked in The Episcopal Church, a Mainline denomination whose membership Pew Research Forum estimates to be 90 percent white and 55 percent women.[5] So on paper at least, it made perfect sense to make this my religious home, particularly after I'd begun to transition and to live a more visibly queer life.

Beyond demographics, Episcopal canon law at the time I was a member further prohibited the denomination from denying any layperson "rights, status or access to an equal place in the life, worship, governance, or employment of this church because of ... sex, sexual orientation, gender identity and expression."[6] Moreover, The Episcopal Church has in recent years made its generally progressive stance on 2SLGBTQ+-inclusion a key element of its public image. This is, after all, the first branch of the global Anglican Communion to consecrate an openly gay bishop, Gene Robinson:[7] the same Gene Robinson who famously wore a bulletproof vest the day he ascended to the See of New Hampshire on account of assassination threats made against him;[8] and who preached at the Washington National Cathedral when Matthew Shepard, the victim of a 1998 anti-gay hate crime,[9] was interred there in 2008. And The Episcopal Church is also the denomination that, in 2018, approved a liturgical "Service of Renaming" for use throughout the church,[10] a development that advocates for the inclusion of trans and nonbinary Episcopalians especially welcomed.[11]

In short, I came honestly to the naïve belief that "The Episcopal Church Welcomes You" meant that The Episcopal Church welcomed me.

That term—naïve—is one typically applied to the inexperienced or the young. I was both, and all too eager to accept that this declining denomination would embrace me as warmly as its marketing suggested.[12]

But though the church's most recognizable modern slogan makes for compelling signage, it is far from an accurate description of on-the-ground realities for those who are unwilling or unable to fit the mold of the ideal Episcopalian at worship: a figure who is straight, white, cisgender, middle- to upper-class, and, importantly, male. Walk through the bright red door, and a litany of qualifications limit whom, exactly, the denomination means when it speaks of "The Episcopal Church;" what, exactly, it means by "Welcomes;" and whom, exactly, it means by "You."

The upshot is that, if a white trans girl like me has any place at all in this denomination of white women, it is a precarious one—even if it is a position that would be more fragile still if my body were racialized, as well.

But I'm getting ahead of myself. After all, this chapter is supposed to have something to do with the devil.

So, for now, let me just tell you a joke:

What does the trans girl call a church that makes her life hell when she's alive, but is progressive enough that its clergy will commend her soul to heaven when she's dead? Episcopalian.

Are you laughing?

III.

Some zingers fit for impolite company:

[If you don't have a pussy] then you are not a woman you fucking idiot. Fuck off freak!!!! Women don't have dicks retard—Scott (or something like that), to me, via Tinder

Fucking faggot you'll never ever be a woman so fucking nasty gross fuck you—Phil, to me, also via Tinder

So you're a tranny?—Zabi, to me, again via (you guessed it!) Tinder

IV.

I've long had sympathy for the devil. And I think it's because I simply find this damned angel so damn hilarious.

I shouldn't, of course. The devil is no laughing matter.

Just ask the New Testament authors. The devil "has been sinning from the beginning," one writer points out, and those who sin are his children (1 John 3:8 NRSV).[13] He has "the power of death," we hear in Hebrews 2:14; and, thus, it was through death that Christ destroyed him and freed those whom fear of death enslaved. Jesus' own condemnation of the devil, in the Gospel of John 8:44, is perhaps the sharpest: The devil "was a murderer from the beginning and does not stand in the truth ... [H]e is a liar and the father of lies." And what will become of this great deceiver, this "ancient serpent" (Revelation 20:2)? If the New Testament's concluding book is any guide, the devil's ultimate fate is to be "thrown into the lake of fire and sulfur" (Revelation 20:10), where eternal agony awaits him.

Ouch.

Nor does the weight of the Christian tradition favour seeing the devil as anything other than a Very Serious Matter that Very Serious Christians ought to take Very Seriously.

Take Robert Jenson's 1989 article "Evil as Person,"[14] a rare example of a contemporary-ish Mainline theologian giving specific, focused attention to the devil and his place as a distinct, personal entity active within the created order. Jenson makes much of the devil's humor, and its deficiencies relative to God's—and our own. The devil "is never truly funny," Jenson insists, because his laughter is always at others, never at himself.[15] Indeed, it was his very inability to "take God's big joke on him and the other great spirits" that precipitated his fall in the first place.[16] He could not see the humor in an angel serving mere animals, *humans*.

So, rather than submit himself with a chuckle to God's foolish scheme at the creation of the world, the devil plunged himself into the shadows, at the cost of his own selfhood. He so resists being the object of laughter—of the humorous gaze of others, and of himself—that if he is "indeed a person," it is "a parasite-person: the laughter which constitutes him a person is always on someone else."[17] In the end, then, Jenson's account makes of the devil a rather pathetic figure: If only the devil were to recognize just how ridiculous he and his actions truly are, the devil might have a self—a self that God would save.

This is where Jenson and I disagree most pointedly. Because unlike him, I have to believe the devil's been laughing at himself from the beginning; that in the grand cosmic drama Christians tell of creation, fall, and redemption, the devil's been saved this whole time. I have to believe it, because when I meditate on the devil's experience, I hear echoes of my own.

And like my own life, the devil's fall from divine favour and the mayhem that ensues has the key marks of a situation comedy—a sitcom.

In her brilliant essay on "Paranoia as a Trans Style," historian and theorist Jules Gill-Peterson observes that situation comedians play with conventionality, "often by recontextualizing a character," to humorous effect. Take some familiar figures, group them together in surprising or unfamiliar ways, throw this motley crew into a series of scenarios, and laugh at their reactions. "The situation comedian understands that the social enmeshment of people uncomfortably—and humorously—makes it impossible to separate them," Gill-Peterson explains, "despite the violence done every day as if those differences are ordained." These people are in it together, and it turns out they—and *we*, the audience whooping along as we watch their misadventures—aren't really so different after all (ha!).[18]

Except that, of course we are. And, at the end of the day, that's the point.

The situation comedy plays with, without finally erasing, the interpersonal distinctions between its cast of characters, and between its cast and the audience for their performance. It thereby resolves these figures into view as individuals-in-collectivities and, in the process, becomes a vehicle for coalition building.

Entries in this genre work because the performers are up there on the stage, but the audience is not. Because it so strains credulity that *these characters*, in all their individual uniqueness, should navigate as a cohort the situations scripted for them. Because the confluence of those particularities yields surprising, at times patently ridiculous, outcomes at which one cannot help but laugh.

Laugh because convention dictates that what one is seeing shouldn't be possible—and, in that laughter, apprehend convention's contingency, the potential to transcend it through novel social formations, the necessity of community for doing so. It is their exploration of such formations that gives the very best situation comedies—the ones with the most political edge and, yes, in many cases the ones that most offend audience sensibilities—their unpredictability. It is also what makes our laughing at them so delightful in its sheer obscenity, the object of that laughter being, ultimately, the norms that govern our experience of the everyday.

And behind every situation comedy lie two choices. There is the cast members' choice to become the joke. And there is the audience's choice to be present for it—the audience's choice, that is, to show up and laugh.

These are the same choices trans people make when we come out. Gill-Peterson again: "Going from a life where the joke's on me and I have no control to the one where I choose to make the joke on me? That's being trans, baby."[19] To which I would add: Making this choice and also giggling about it? That's gender euphoria, baby.

The choice to be trans is a choice to be both the joke and the audience in a situation comedy that makes a mockery of contemporary life and the hierarchical politics that make that life available to some but deny it to most.

It is a choice to live in a world hostile to your existence; to be hated; to be driven from the spaces one tries to inhabit; to experience an unending torrent of ridicule and jeers. And yet, seemingly paradoxically, it is also a choice to experience a special kind of joy, a joy that flows from the queer alchemy of exile and desire.

Aren't these the very choices the devil makes at his fall?

V.

In the beginning, the devil sinned.

All angels are pure spirit, whom God created originally good. And the devil, being an angel himself, was no different. But he and those angels we now call demons "became evil by their own doing."

In their own free will, they chose to "radically and irrevocably" reject God and God's heavenly kingdom. Envy was the motivation for this decision, death its effect. And like the dead who did not convert in life, repentance is unavailable to the devil and his demonic companions. They committed an "unforgivable" sin.

Thus did the devil fall, according to The Catechism of the Catholic Church.[20]

VI.

Choices—the Christian life is full of them.

None of those choices are entirely the Christian's own. God's providential governance of the cosmos is such that the divine hand is always present in the happenings of our lives: impelling us to act; staying our impulses; on a grander scale, orchestrating the ebb and flow of history's currents.

Still, some choices are more ours than others. The decision to make a personal commitment to Jesus Christ as lord and savior would be one. If I do it, I do it myself; no one does it for me, nor could they. Another example is the decision to adopt a particular Christian tradition as one's own: whether formally, through a rite of confirmation or the like; informally, through regular participation in that tradition's corporate worship; or some combination of the two. Yet another is to seek God's forgiveness when one sins, and to thank God for the blessings of this life. And it is, finally, within one to elect to be married within the Church; to seek the Church's comfort when one is sick; and, when the time comes, to will one's burial from it.

But many of the choices that most define Christians are not ones that Christians themselves make. Those baptized as babies, for instance, do not decide to be; their parents and church community make this decision on their behalf. Moving beyond the early years of life: while one might choose to make Anglicanism their denominational home, say, they do not choose its commitments or contents; the tradition chooses these for them, and the individual inherits the legacy of the past. In a similar vein, while one might have certain wishes as to what should happen to their body after their death, even if they dictate those wishes in a legal will they are in no position to enforce them; in the end, it will be others who determine what becomes of their remains.

In many Christian accounts of the afterlife, damnation is just another choice. One that, in a popular solution to the "problem of hell," certain people ultimately make for themselves.

The problem of hell is closely related to the problem of evil, and its resolution is a kind of theodicy. How is it possible, the challenge goes, that a good and loving God separates people "from the presence of the Lord and from the glory of his might" in a place of "eternal destruction" (2 Thessalonians 1:9)? The answer: God doesn't. For whatever reason, some people just prefer hell to heaven, and God honors their decision. End of story.

It's a tidy solution that skillfully absolves God of any responsibility for the afterlife of, presumably, intense and unending misery to which the damned fate themselves.

Maybe they heard a poor articulation of the gospel news, or they never heard it at all; and so others decided their eternal destiny for them. Maybe it doesn't matter whether they accept God's offer of salvation in this life, because it remains open for them to do so in the next; however, by the time they arrive, a lifetime of wrongdoing has so warped their souls that the damned can't but hide from the divine presence. Either way, if they end up in hell, that's not really on God.

But what if the problem of hell were no problem at all?

What if some people make hell their posthumous home not because they are ignorant of heaven, or by some personal defect unable to experience its glory; but because, with full awareness of who God is and direct experience of what a fully consummated relationship with him entails, they simply judge hell to be better?

That is, after all, what the devil does at his fall. And it's quite frankly amusing.

We're talking about a pure spirit who had beheld the very face of the Father (Matthew 18:10), but elected expulsion from the divine presence anyways. An angel who chose to prowl the earth as the enemy of God's holy people (1 Peter 5:8), like all people created in God's very image. A person who willingly departed the heavenly lights and gained bondage in the darkness of hell (Jude 6); as well as the nothingness, the utter disintegration of the self, that is the fate of those who dwell therein.

The devil and his cadre of demonic allies looked upon the Beatific Vision itself and said, "Nah."

So is it any wonder, then, that when I hear tales of the devil's fall, I can't keep myself from giggling? I mean, *come on*. What the hell kind of choice is that? A pretty comical one, if you ask me.

But also one that, I have to believe, the devil and those angels that follow him are right to make.

VII.

Here's a joke you can tell all your Episcopal friends. You know, the ones who don't check their brains at the door on Sunday mornings.

A tranny walks into her parish church. 2SLGBTQ+ Pride flags are visible everywhere, and the priest makes a point during public worship of reminding attendees that God welcomes everyone to her table.

"Excellent!," the tranny thinks to herself. So she makes this her church home, and even gets involved in leading some of its ministries.

But the tranny soon learns the priest's reputation for misogyny and transphobia is an open secret amongst long-time congregants. And soon she experiences both herself.

The priest forces the tranny from her leadership positions, publicly mocks her and her gender identity, puts her church friends in the position of having to choose between supporting her or the one who stands before them each week in the person of Christ, and reduces her mental health to tatters. So the tranny leaves.

After the dust has settled, the tranny asks the priest for an apology. She is denied.

So she calls the bishop, and asks him to order the priest to apologize. But she is denied again.

Finally, she asks the diocese to provide her with the pastoral care her priest never did. And a third time she is denied.

Has it all been a waste? No, the tranny is told, for "deep listening and learning" has occurred.

To which the tranny replies: "With friends like these, who needs episcopacy?"

VIII.

We do not choose the world.

It comes to us as the product of others' decisions: in the first place, of God's choice to speak it into being; in the second, of our ancestors' choice to fashion creation as they have. Through no actions of our own, we are born into a world of inequalities, violence, and strife. And regardless of whether its structures advantage or disadvantage us, that world is the gift God and history offers to each of us—a gift we have no choice but to accept, at least for a little while, even though doing so means, for most of us, accepting foreshortened lives and premature deaths.

But while we might not decide *to* inhabit this world of ours, having now arrived it is to a significant degree within our power to determine the *manner* in which we do so. Heirs of the world, what we do with our inheritance is for us to decide. And in making those decisions, we inheritors—we future ancestors—undertake our own projects of world-making.

These are projects of "inclusion."

The term is one that self-styled "liberal" white Christians, particularly in the Mainline, are fond of bandying about when the existence of trans-identifying people comes up. "Such-and-such denomination now permits these folks to minister at the altar and preach from the pulpit," a familiar line of progressive rhetoric runs. "Look at how inclusive that church is!"

Never mind that few of the people supposedly included in the denomination's corporate life might actually participate in any of the church's functions; that the ones who do might not stick around for very long; or that those who attain positions of power and authority might also principally be the ones most able to assimilate themselves into, and reproduce the structures and mores of, the denomination's dominant social classes.

This way of conceptualizing inclusion emphasizes the inheritance offered, but without caring much about whether the inheritors who supposedly benefit most directly from it actually receive it at all. A church is inclusive, this thinking goes, if its doors are open to trans people—if, that is, members of this coalition have unrestricted access to the riches of the denomination's traditions—even if that's only true on paper (just look at the signs!). "Inclusion" becomes synonymous with "welcome."

And once inclusion is granted, and welcome extended, the work is done. Inclusive Christians can turn their attention to the injustices that the included experience outside the church's walls, and need not speak at all to the injustices trans people continue to experience within them. Insofar as trans people are welcome they are also, by virtue of this fact, included—it's entirely unnecessary for any of these people to actually be around come Sunday morning, or to be safe from transphobic bigotries if they are.

Inclusion looks rather different if, instead, we take the view that it begins and ends with the presence of the included themselves.

A space is *de facto* inclusive whenever these people inhabit it; whether anyone else consents to, or is happy about, their being there is irrelevant. And that space ceases to be inclusive of these people when it ceases to accommodate them; their absence marks their exclusion. Unwelcome, uninvited, out-of-place—the excluded show up, inserting themselves into places where, as a matter of right, they do not belong, and thereby make those spaces inclusive as a matter of fact.

The devil's fall is just such an act of inclusivity.

The Hebrew and Christian Scriptures give us few details about this event, making the devil's fall and the circumstances that surrounded it fertile ground for theological speculation. What we do know is that the devil departed from heaven—"like a flash of lightning," Jesus teaches in Luke 10:18. And that this occurred, if Isaiah 14:12–15 is any guide, because the devil said in his heart that he would "make [himself] like the Most High," a resolution that led to his being "brought down to Sheol, to the depths of the Pit."

Commentators—Christian ones, especially—have tended to interpret the devil's desire for godlikeness as pride, this figure's subsequent plummet into the depths as God's righteous judgment on a deviant angel. For reasons rooted in my theology of creation, I myself prefer to tread a different path: one that discerns in the devil's flight from paradise an almost-unintelligible form of worship.

If God alone fashioned the heavens and the earth, as the Scriptural witness of the Christian and Hebrew traditions makes clear (see, e.g., Prov 3:19; Jeremiah 10:12–13; John 1:3), then this world is a given for the devil just as it is for us. The devil, too, is a creature who owes his very existence to the divine Creator (Ezekiel 28:13). And as a creature, it is beyond the devil's abilities to create from nothing; the power to do so is God's, "who alone stretched out the heavens and trampled the waves of the Sea; who made the Bear and Orion, the Pleiades and the chambers of the south" (Job 9:8–9).

So while the devil fell to the earth, he did not make the earth. Instead, he inherited something that God had already set into motion; a place created not as a wasteland, but as a domain God "formed ... to be inhabited" (Isaiah 45:18).

Inhabited by whom? Creatures, to be sure: the birds of the air, the fish of the sea, and vegetation of all kinds. But, more particularly, by God's image-bearers: humans, created "according to [God's] likeness" and tasked with "fill[ing] the earth and subdu[ing] it" (Genesis 1:26, 28).

Earth is the image-bearers' domain, their proper home. Which is why the Christian hope is not of transcending the world, but rather of experiencing its final perfection: the time when, as Revelation 21 describes, heaven and earth will come together and "the home of God [will be] among mortals." But until that hope is realized, the earth as it exists now is where those who bear God's likeness properly belong. Upon its face we humans make our finite lives until, at death, we "return to the ground, for out of it [we] were taken; [we] are dust, and to dust [we] shall return" (Genesis 3:19).

The devil, in heaven at the moment of creation, did not elect this state of affairs. But we have some idea about how he elected to respond to it: by cultivating a desire for godlikeness, which is nothing other than a desire to image God as humans do by nature. This creature wanted to shine with the face of its Creator. And if earth is where the creatures who do just that reside, what would it mean for God to grant the devil's wish but to send him out of heaven?

I am convinced, in other words, that the devil fell not out of pride, but out of devotion. His ascent "to the tops of the clouds" (Isaiah 14:14) was a successful bid to include himself and his comrade angels amongst the divine image-bearers, and it necessitated his subsequent descent to the earth where he would be amongst those who from birth enjoy a godlike form.

Earth became more inclusive as a result of the devil's choice to image God in an abnormal fashion—not as a human but as an angel, as pure spirit. And that choice initiated a project of world-making the end result of which is hell.

But all this came at a terrible cost. Violence is the predictable response of those who normatively inhabit a space at the appearance of those who do not. And this is true for the devil's fall. That event continues to elicit militant opposition from Christians who have never needed to make the decision that precipitated it, because Christians' mode of imaging God—that is, as humans—aligns without effort with the structures of the world that preexist their own creation.

To include himself amongst those who would work to exclude him: that was the devil's choice at creation. And it is a choice trans people—among them trans women in The Episcopal Church—make every day.

IX.

In the beginning, the devil shared in the light in which all the saints participate.

God created him without blemish, but his was a purity that could be lost—as, indeed, is the purity of all save the Trinity. And the devil strayed, departing from righteousness and justice and meriting censure.

So far from goodness did the devil venture that he converted himself into an opposing power, losing the name Lucifer and becoming an enemy of God. Plummeting from heaven to earth, the devil assumed power over all those who submitted to his wickedness. And like all the wicked, the devil's glory transformed into dust.

Thus did the devil fall, according to Origen.

X.

If you want to know about the devil, you need to know about jokes. And trans women tell the *funniest* jokes.

I suppose that's why cis people always seem to be laughing at us. Why they'll snicker as we walk past them on the sidewalk; call us faggots with huge grins on their faces; and hoot with delight as another caricature of the proverbial "man in a dress"—sporting a comically large Adam's apple, a baritone voice, and two-day beard stubble—trots across their television screens.

We're a punchline that never gets old.

Until we're not, that is. And as a trans woman, you don't have to work very hard to experience firsthand the fleetingness of cis laughter. Just try to use the same bathrooms they do, or play in their sports leagues. Or do something a cis man could—maybe, possibly, with sufficient interpretive leaps—construe as signaling a predatory sexual desire for him. Or simply wear too many of white femininity's accoutrements. Suddenly the smiles vanish; the laughter ceases and accusations of fetishism take its place; anger, rejection, violence, and even murder become live possibilities.[21]

This isn't true for *all* cis people, of course. There are those who would *never* laugh at a tranny like me; who recognize how deeply *inappropriate* it is when other people do; and who are prepared, as *allies*, to call out transphobic humor when they hear it. Their laughter isn't so much fleeting as non-existent.

But these folks are the exception that proves the rule: that the trouble with cis people isn't *that* they laugh at trans folks; it's that they don't laugh at us nearly often enough. If only they did, the cis-ies of the world might transition themselves!

Indeed, some of the most oppressively serious spaces I inhabit as a trans woman are those progressive Christian ones in which cis people committed to my "liberation" predominate.

Because, here, liberation tends to mean assimilation: granting some of us the accoutrements of power and privilege so that the rest of us will fall in line, learn to behave ourselves, and like good Episcopalians strive after a bishop's miter and a nice house in Dupont Circle.

It means fighting over whether to permit trans people to discern ordination to Holy Orders within The Episcopal Church—permission General Convention only formally affirmed in 2012—without critically reflecting on the ways in which The Episcopal Church's ordination processes, employment structures, and clerical hierarchy are fundamentally hostile to, especially, the trans women who access them.[22] Because the goal is not to challenge the system that perpetuates cis-masculine dominance, the one that ensures 60 percent of the church's paid USA-based clergy are male while only 45 percent of its total membership is.[23] It is to ensure that the only trans women with anything approximating institutional prominence are the ones who keep that system alive.

Here, liberation means Bishop Robinson declaring in a February 7, 2021, address at Washington National Cathedral that "while a lot of us [2SLGBTQ+ people] are still in pain, while a lot of us have experienced some awful things in our lives, we've won."[24] And it means Robinson doing so mere moments after the Cathedral gave its pulpit to evangelical pastor Max Lucado, who in 2004 suggested publicly that legalizing same-sex marriage was a gateway to the legalization of polygamy or incest.[25] Because Robinson seemingly *has* won. So, therefore, the rest of us must have won, too. Time to sit quietly and include people, like Lucado, "who we don't agree with much at all."

Liberation in these spaces means turning us trannies into the polite cis-ies who have so graciously invited us into the fold.

And in order for that to occur, the cis-ies must make us feel like we belong and are safe in their churches. But since, in the end, we don't and we aren't, the assimilative project gives rise to a culture of hypervigilance. Our progressive liberators must always be on the lookout for the things that would give away their game, like the laughter that would disclose the extent to which they will always regard us as abnormalities to be cured; and, until that happens, as comical parodies of their norms.

Don't tell a trans joke! If you do, we trannies might realize we *are* the joke—albeit not one cis-ies want to tell—and leave. And if we leave, how will the cis-ies liberate us from our transness and bring about the utopia of a world without our presence?

How, you might ask, will they exorcize us? As Christians are so fond of exorcizing the devil, driving him from the face of the earth and the bodies he indwells into the darkness of hell.

I don't know to what extent this disgraced angel foresaw the consequences of his fall. Whether he knew in advance the suffering for which he was fating himself, or the violence he would be made to endure. Somehow I doubt that, finite creature that he is, the devil could have had more than a partial grasp of what lay ahead.

But if his future was uncertain at his departure from heaven, it has surely become all-too clear with each passing day. Each day he is cast out of the earthly spaces in which he tries to make his home; each day the world's evils are pinned on him and his seductions; each day he is hated, despised, and made to more closely resemble nothing at all by those who worship the God in whose presence the devil once stood.

And yet, in what is surely one of Christianity's great mysteries, the devil persists in his exile; in his sojourning "to and fro on the earth" (Job 1:7); in his efforts to recruit humanity to his cause. If "the doors of hell are locked on the inside," as C.S. Lewis wrote in *The Great Divorce*, why does the devil not open them and return to the garden of heavenly delights?[26]

Perhaps because—amidst all the pain, the rejection, and the unfulfilled longing to belong on the earth; indeed, maybe *because* of all that—the devil still finds it within himself to laugh. And it is Christians who don't recognize that laughter for what it is, or do so only with great difficulty, because they do not have the ears to hear.

The devil's fall was not, after all, a once-and-for-all occurrence. If heaven remains a live option for him—and, indeed, for all those who cohabitate hell with him—then his continued refusals to return to it reiterate that original fall from glory. Every time the devil chooses hell, he falls again; his plunge into the depths continues; the event remains temporally present, resisting slippage into the past.

If the devil makes this decision knowing full well what awaits him, having made the choice before and experienced the consequences, surely there must be a delight in damnation; in remaining beyond redemption, at least for now. Surely this hell the devil is fashioning for himself, with all the damned, must have its own kind of beauty: a beauty born of expulsion and an unfulfilled yearning to belong elsewhere.

I have to believe as much, in any event. For transitioning is a similar choice, one similarly locked in a perpetual present tense, that the world finds similarly incomprehensible. And when you've lived long enough in a body the world demonizes, the demonic doesn't seem all that bad.

I choose to be a trans woman in a world that hates trans women. I choose this every day, with increasing knowledge and experience of the panoply of methods by which this world wears trans women down and eventually sends us to our early graves. Whatever ignorance I might have been able to claim when I first came out has evaporated with the passage of time. And yet, although the option to detransition is always there, I still decide every morning to get up, put on makeup and a skirt, and live as Charlotte knowing the penalty for doing so is a slow death.

And that, indeed, is the least intelligible part of transitioning male-to-female: we trans women bring hatred, violence, and death upon ourselves. We choose it. Not because we built this world that's so inhospitable to our presence, but because we elect to inhabit it *as trans women* all the same.

I can't speak to every trans woman's reasons for doing so, but I can speak to mine: I choose this because of the joy, the pleasure, the *laughter* I've found in going through life as the world's big gag. Because I find it so patently ridiculous, so utterly delightful, that this unusual woman that I am should be here at all. Because, most days, I look forward to the jokes I can tell, to the jokes that cis people will tell me, knowing that the line between us is one good chuckle from being overcome. Most days.

And so, in the end, I have to sympathize with the devil. And I have to insist to myself that however much Christians might do to push him away, not even he is beyond the redemption they have already secured, not ultimately. Because if he's not, then maybe, in the end, neither am I.

That's pretty funny, too, when you think about it.

XI.

In the beginning, God creates the devil a pure spirit and welcomes her into the divine presence.

When, at the creation of the world, God creates humanity in the divine image, the devil comes before her Maker. "These mortals image you," she begins. "In your mercy, permit me to bear your image, too."

And God grants the devil's request. "But if this is your wish," God explains, "you must depart. For earth is the home of my image bearers, and that is what you shall be." So God sends the devil out from heaven, along with all those who share in her desire; and they make their home amongst humans.

But whenever the devil takes physical form, it horrifies the saints. When she attempts to commune with them, it fills Christians with dread. When she speaks, they hear only curses and expressions of pain.

Abused, displaced, excluded, feared—the devil and her demonic friends retreat to a new home in the depths, where they welcome all those who recognize in these angels the face of God.

Seeing this, and feeling the extent of the devil's pain, God every day calls down to her in her sunken abode. "My saints despise and dread you," God tells her, "and drive you out of their holy places. Live in infamy no longer," God pleads; "return to heaven and again take your place amongst the angels who share in my light."

But the pain of the devil's longing is the pain of a futile hope, and it is a balm to she who knows the depths of agony reserved for those who have abandoned longing altogether. In hell alone do the hopes of the damned persist, rising from their lips as laughter that reaches the very ear of the Father. And so, every day, the devil hears the word of the Lord and answers: "No."

Thus does the devil fall, according to me.

PART FIVE
Hope, Naïveté

The most debilitating thing wasn't the hallucinations or the delusions, although neither of those helped. It was the memory problems.

One day, sometime in the summer after my second year of law school, I forgot where I lived.

I was walking down the street, fleeing the people I knew to be after me. (I'm supposed to tell you this is a delusion.) I found myself on a street that ought to have been familiar, and I didn't know where I was. Everything looked so strange.

I was lost—in my city, in my mind.

━━━━━━

Psychosis is a thief.[1] When it comes, it steals my world.

And when I sat down to write these words, it had been coming a lot.

Not the way it used to, before I went on my meds. I wasn't hearing voices out of the silence, at least, not very often. But I still believed things I was told were delusions, even if I mostly knew that that's what they were. And from time to time I would even do things like try to cut out the tracker I knew "they" had put in my arm. I still believed my delusions enough that I was willing to bleed for them.

This was a problem. But it was not *the* problem.

The problem was that psychosis is a thief that doesn't come alone.

━━━━━━

My memory problems began—in the sense that I first started noticing them—around the same time my psychotic episodes became disabling. I'm convinced the two are related in some way—it's too much of a coincidence to be a coincidence.[2]

And the problems became steadily worse.

I would forget conversations. I would forget whether I had eaten, or what I had done the previous week. I could not keep instructions in my mind long enough to execute them, not even when it was something as simple as remembering to get sugar from the pantry moments after reading an ingredients list in a recipe.

I just could not remember anymore.

For a while—a painfully long time—my doctors could not tell me why this was the case. And that was just as frustrating as the memory problems themselves.

Because I was sure, at the time, that it was another thing my illness had stolen from me.

For a while, I lived in a kind of eternal present. Once a moment was gone, unless I had taken some step to record it, it was gone for good.

I had no choice but to live in the here and now. And there was nothing romantic about it. Because the moments I forgot were the moments that make up a life.

At the time, I thought that maybe, one day, when I was "better" at last, I would remember those moments again. Or at least know why I had forgotten them in the first place.

And I was right.

Ten

A FUTURE FOR EVE

IN GENESIS 3:20, ADAM addresses his wife, renaming her. He had previously called her *"'ishshah,"* woman, "for from man was she taken" (JPS). But having eaten from the tree of the knowledge of good and evil, Adam and Eve stand before God, cursed (see Genesis 3:16-19). And Eve stands before her husband, who renames her *Chava*, "the mother of all the living."

But that wasn't all Adam said. The rabbis of the sixth-century CE Midrashic text *Bereshit Rabbah* tell us that, in the moment of naming, "Adam the first man told her how many generations she had caused to perish."[1] Life and death intermingle in this moment. Eve will be a mother to all, true—but a mother to all who die.

We mortals are Eve's children. And her curse is ours, too.

The Cursed of the Earth

Of the ritual books for sale by the United States Conference of Catholic Bishops, only one must be purchased through a local bishop. *Exorcisms and Related Supplications* is the official English-language translation of the Roman Catholic Church's rite of major exorcism.[2] Published in 2017, some twenty years after the Vatican released the first substantial revision of its Latin exorcism liturgy since 1614, the text's fifty-odd pages of prayers and Scripture readings equip bishop- and priest-exorcists to deliver members of the Christian faithful from demonic possession.

In the first of two supplementary appendices, an additional seven pages outline the procedure exorcists are to follow when demonic entities penetrate places and objects or otherwise persecute the Church (what are known as *minor* exorcisms). And if a lay Catholic feels they are a target of the devil's assaults, but do not require a proper exorcism, there are resources for this person, too. These take the form of a second appendix containing "Supplications which may be used by the faithful privately in their struggle against the power of darkness," the only section of the book that is publicly available.

But if a copy of *Exorcisms and Related Supplications* is uniquely difficult to obtain, a Roman Catholic exorcism is not. By all accounts, in fact, the number of exorcisms is on the rise both in the United States and globally—so much so that, in 2005, the Vatican launched a special course to train would-be exorcists in the theory and practice of combatting malevolent supernatural agents.[3]

Generally speaking, the Roman Catholic Church reserves its rite of major exorcism for baptized Roman Catholics who suffer, as the preface to *Exorcisms and Related Supplications* puts it, "with God's permission, ... [from] particular torment or possession which the devil inflicts." As one Vatican-educated exorcist explained to me, this restriction is both pragmatically as well as theologically motivated: until a person is baptized, Satan has a legitimate claim to their soul and body; and this claim makes it substantially less likely that any diabolical agents possessing them will recognize and submit to the authority the Roman Catholic Church exercises in its ministry of exorcism. The Roman Catholic Church has nonetheless acknowledged the ecumenical need for Christian ministers skilled in this ministry, and, in 2019, began admitting members of other Christian denominations to its "Exorcism and Prayer of Liberation Course."

While minor exorcisms feature in The Episcopal Church's baptismal liturgy—baptizands are asked to "renounce Satan and all the spiritual forces of wickedness that rebel against God;" and the Celebrant prays that God would liberate those professing their faith "from the way of sin and death"—Anglicans in the United States have been comparatively less invested than their

Roman Catholic counterparts in defining and disseminating protocols for handling cases of possession that transpire after Christian initiation.[4] The Episcopal Church's *Book of Occasional Services (2018)* treats of major exorcism in a brief section, instructing those "in need of" the rite to consult a bishop by way of their local priest. "The bishop [is] then [to] determine whether exorcism is needed, who is to officiate at the rite, and what prayers or other formularies are to be used."[5] In practice, these instructions mean that how Episcopalians handle instances of demonic possession varies materially from diocese to diocese. One bishop I spoke to, for example, favors the creation of bespoke exorcism liturgies to meet the unique pastoral needs of each demon-afflicted person. While another diocese maintains a team of specialists, trained in the identification and expulsion of demonic agents, to deploy as needed.

I was 22 years old and still aspiring to the Anglican priesthood when I was first called upon to assist with a rite of exorcism. Someone had cursed a parishioner's house, my priest supervisor on the Standing Rock Mission explained to me, and the bishop had authorized us to cleanse the home of demonic entities. So late in the day, the sun sinking low in the South Dakota sky, we drove an hour across the prairie to the remote house: armed with our prayer books, our Holy Communion kit, and our faith in a God who delivers.

The Book of Occasional Services is not entirely without its own minor exorcism liturgy, although it does not bill the rite in such terms. Instead, the text folds exorcistic prayers into its "Celebration for a Home," a ritualized procession that begins in the living room. Participants gather there for an opening collect; readings from Scripture; and, "when appropriate," an invocation that calls forth "the mighty power of the Holy God [to] be present in this place to banish from it every unclean spirit, to cleanse it from every residue of evil, and to make it a secure habitation for *those* who *dwell* in it."[6] The presider then guides the home's inhabitants through the dwelling's individual spaces, leading them in prayers that God would be present within each one.

This two-step process—of casting out the demonic and inviting in the Divine—recalls Jesus' warning in the Gospel of Matthew. There, he cautions that an unclean spirit, having been driven from a person, will return; and, finding its sometime residence "unoccupied, swept clean and put in order," will re-inhabit that individual in the company of "seven other spirits more wicked than itself" (Matthew 12:44–45 NIV). It is not enough, in other words, simply to banish the demonic's personal manifestations if, in so doing, one leaves a place vacant. For the unoccupied space, however clean and orderly its interior might be for a moment, remains a viable site of demonic infestation; and on the demons' return in greater numbers, "the last state of the person is worse than the first" (Matthew 12:45). One must take the further step of filling the place to which those demons staked their claim with a presence capable of keeping them at bay—which is to say, Christians insist, one must claim the space for the Kingdom of God.

Thus it is for people. And the reason why in Holy Baptism, for instance, asking baptizands to renounce Satan is not an end in itself, but merely a prelude to God's bringing them into the communion of saints through water and the movement of the Spirit. Thus is it, too, for the homes Christians inhabit, as the service of "Celebration for a Home" affirms by way of its liturgical structure.

The particular home to which we were called on that warm summer evening sat alone on a large swath of countryside. And as soon as we crossed the fence that demarcated the property from the open prairie that surrounded it, I felt a crushing sense of unease—like a heavy weight on my chest—come over me. Not wanting to appear afraid, however, I told no one of it. Arriving at the home, we commenced the exorcistic liturgy at once, cleansing each room in the home with prayers and holy water in turn. As we moved deeper into the house, towards what we had been told was the most cursed room of all, my sense of unease only grew more profound. The air was thick with fear, the walls pulsed in the all-too inadequate lighting, and still we continued to recite our prayers and sprinkle our holy water. Until, finally, we had blessed the whole house, and the unease instantly lifted. We had succeeded, I was sure of it, but I shared my conviction with no one.

In providing for the exorcism of domiciles, The Episcopal Church grants that to be a Christian is no guarantee of freedom from demonic assault; indeed, that it is within the power of Satan's agents to gain a purchase on that most familiar of places, believers' homes. But the church concedes as much agonistically, affirming diabolical might so as the better to contest it. For such is the promise of an exorcistic rite, that, in the face of evil's manifestations, Christians have recourse to the received tradition of their branch of the church catholic. Provided, of course, that those same believers first recognize their need for such aid; which is to say, recognize as such those situations in which they are dealing with malicious supernatural forces beyond their individual power to overcome.

Insofar as the prescription it offers implies a diagnosis, the "Celebration for a Home" itself guides those familiar with its contents to this moment of recognition. Codifying The Episcopal Church's remedy for cases of demonic infestation, the text invites Episcopalians to presume with it that such events occur with sufficient frequency to warrant a defined, institutional response. So banal is the experience of encountering, and combatting, demons in one's home—the liturgy implies—that it does not even warrant a special service. When praying God's blessing over a home, individual Episcopalians should consequently prepare themselves, as a matter of course, to drive Satan's legions from the space first; after all, if not they, then a number of their siblings in Christ, have found it necessary to do so.

"Celebration for a Home" in this way creates its own necessity. Be vigilant, it warns; demons might well be occupying your abode. Watch out! They might even be occupying your body, or attempting to—if, that is, the parallelism between home and body is as my reading suggests.

There is nothing especially mysterious or spectacular about the service of "Celebration for a Home." Demons register within it, but as seemingly quotidian entities—creatures it is often necessary to dispatch, but procedurally, as a prelude to performing the task ultimately at hand. And, in this case, that task is to call forth—as one of the prayers reads—"the gladness of [God's] presence." It is to delight, you might otherwise say, in the glory of God as it manifests in the spaces of our lives; rather than to dwell on those things that will to keep us from doing so.

Demonology is, simply, the science of parsing evil through sustained attention to evil's personal manifestations. Christian rites of exorcism advance this work insofar as they communicate the Church's understanding of the place those manifestations occupy within the world, generally, and the Christian life, particularly. This is so whether those rites come as standalone liturgies, like the ones contained in *Exorcisms and Related Supplications*; or exorcistic elements within larger wholes, like "Celebration for a Home." In neither example is there any doubt about whether the Church, intervening on Christians' behalf against whatever wickedness besets them, will prevail against the gates of hell: When Christians prayerfully contest demonic power, regardless of the domain within which they do so, their victory—which is, ultimately, God's victory—is preordained. And it is this understanding of evil, as not simply ubiquitous but as everywhere already defeated, that exorcistic liturgies, major and minor, disseminate amongst the faithful.

The Roman Catholic Rite of Major Exorcism is in this respect exemplary. Beginning softly, with the priest-exorcist offering a quiet prayer to invoke divine protection, the service soon reaches a suitably dramatic liturgical crescendo. When the time arrives for the exorcist to cast the devil out of the possessed person, two sorts of prayers are available. The first, "Deprecative Formulae," are a mandatory component of the liturgy. Addressed to God, these call upon the Almighty, as one such formula puts it, "to deliver this your servant from all the power of the infernal spirits." Prayers of the second sort, "Imperative Formulae," are optional and address the devil directly. "I exorcize you, ancient foe of mankind," one begins; going on to command Satan to "depart in the name of Jesus Christ, the mighty one who cast you out by the finger of God and destroyed your kingdom."

There is manifest confidence in these utterances, and reasonably so. For, in exorcizing the demon possessed, the Church acts from a position of strength that is grounded in hope: the hope that, in the end, there are no dark places for the Father of Heavenly Lights.

Our Celebration for a Home on Standing Rock ended with a service of Holy Communion, after which we debriefed the ritual as a whole with the family whose home it was and the Indigenous Elder who had accompanied us on our exorcistic journey. Had we succeeded, the family wanted to know? Yes, the Elder replied firmly. For when he had first arrived on the property, he felt a crushing sense of unease that only intensified as our rite unfolded; but, once we had exorcized the whole house, that unease had lifted in an instant.

The Second Naïveté

Paul Ricoeur was among the twentieth century's great theorists of textual interpretation. And in *The Symbolism of Evil*,[7] he writes of two naïvetés.

The first is the almost childlike naïveté of those who take religious myths—be they expressed in doctrine or in Scriptural stories—at face value and believe them to be true without thought or reflection. Criticism—be it historical, literary, theoretical, or theological—destroys these naïve beliefs, exposing them to be false. And some people never get beyond the wreckage that remains, disbelieving everything their religion taught them because it is all *prima facie* incompatible with rational thought. But some move on.

The "second naïveté" is achieved "in and through criticism."[8] Religious myths cease to be explanations for the world and, instead, become symbols—metaphors that guide interpretation and allow us to "hear again."[9]

Interpreting these myths is no longer a matter of simply accepting what religious functionaries tell us that they mean, and is instead a matter of finding ways for them to speak to us *in light of our critical thinking about them*. "This second naïveté," Ricoeur thus writes, "aims to be the postcritical equivalent of the precritical hierophany."[10] We choose to believe in order that we might understand, and we understand insofar as we believe.

Critical interpretation becomes a "restorative" rather than a "reductive" endeavour,[11] reconstructive instead of deconstructive.

Losing Faith, Finding Home

I "lost" my Christian faith sometime shortly after I graduated from Yale. I had seen the way those in positions of institutional power within Christian churches abuse the vulnerable; during my last year of seminary, I had become the target of some of those abuses. Growing up, I had been taught that once you accept Christ Jesus as your personal lord and savior, he would lead you to holiness. The fact that some of the people who most vocally proclaimed Christ's saving grace were doing the abusing behind closed doors—and sometimes in front of them—shattered that belief. If Jesus was as alive and active as Christians insisted, how could Christian leaders perpetrate so much evil in Jesus' name?

On my return home to Western Canada, I fell in with a local Jewish community. It wasn't an accident. At Yale, some of the most faithful and thoughtful people I knew were Jews themselves; they were also among the most committed to critical thought and rational inquiry in matters of God. If these were Jews, I reasoned, I wanted to spend more time with them.

So I started attending *Shabbat* services. I started observing Jewish festivals. I started stumbling through Hebrew prayers. Not because I wanted new ways to encounter God—I could not care less about God, if I'm being honest—but because I wanted as many ways as possible to encounter Jewish people.

You can find God anywhere, if you look closely enough. But good people? They're harder to locate. In the end, I found them at what became my synagogue.

Conversion to Judaism is something of an arduous process.[12] At my synagogue, you need to pray with the community for at least a year, take a class on the basics of Jewish practices and beliefs, and then appear before a rabbinical court (*Beit Din*) that determines whether to admit you to the House of Israel. My own conversion took three years, interrupted as it was by a year of florid psychosis in which everything in my life—school, work, and, yes, organized religion—stopped.

Once the *Beit Din* had approved my conversion, before I undertook the ritual of immersion that would officially mark my entrance into the Jewish community, I was asked to select a Hebrew name for myself. I already knew my answer: *Chava.*

Eve was, after all, a woman who had been created from a man, like me. She is one widely despised, by Christians in particular, but who can nonetheless claim with a special kind of literalness to be a child of God. And in taking her name, this is a woman who finds her own kind of future in me, an heir to her curse but also, in my own way, to her promise: to be a mother to all the living. For if you sustain a life, it is as if you sustain an entire world, the *Talmud* teaches.[13] And in choosing to convert to Judaism, I was choosing to sustain my life, spiritually as well as physically. I was deciding to make the Jewish story *my* story, and to accept as true even if not as fact the Scriptural basis for that story. I was choosing to be naïve again.

The Devils in Our Midst

These days, I identify more with the demons we exorcized that summer evening than with the priest who led the exorcistic charge. After all, Christians demonize the devil and her legions in much the same way that they demonize trans women and others who have "fallen" into sin. I, too, know what it is like to be driven out of the Christian homes I have tried to call my own. I don't have to wonder what it's like to be cursed by God or by the Church. I don't have to ponder whether Christians can succeed in driving out the "demons" amongst them. I know what it's like to be me.

One of the most common misconceptions about schizophrenia and related psychotic illnesses is that they are fundamentally untreatable. That could not be further from the truth, of course, but the myth persists. True, schizophrenia is a progressively degenerating illness, meaning that with each episode a little more of a person's mind is lost. But it is possible to halt that progression with early intervention, therapeutic doses of antipsychotics, and psychological treatments like cognitive behavioral therapy for psychosis.[14]

I have been fortunate enough to benefit from all of those interventions. Even so, from time to time, the psychosis returns. And when it does, the devil returns with it.

These days, I think of the devil as a kind of recurrent conversation partner. Hearing his voice or believing him to be inserting thoughts into my mind is one of the surest signs that my schizophrenia is returning in acute form, true. But he is also, in his own way, a kind of companion in my travels—in his company, I never have to be alone.

I have often thought of giving my life story an abrupt ending. Sometimes the devil and his hallucinatory entourage encourage me to do so. And there have been many reasons, over the years, why I have not. It would devastate my friends and family, for one. If I tried to do so and failed, I would almost certainly end up hospitalized, and my few experiences of psychiatric detention make that a more fearsome outcome in my mind than winding up on the wrong side of the heaven/hell divide.

But I think the thing that has kept me going the most is hope: hope that, in the end, my story can still have a happier ending than the one my illness would seem to dictate for me.

There is an idea in Judaism, captured most prominently in the Passover Seder, of an eternal Exodus from Egypt. A particularly poignant meditation from the prayerbook (*Siddur*) of my Reform tradition reads,

We are a people in whom the past endures,
In whom the present is inconceivable
  without moments gone by.
The Exodus lasted a moment, a moment enduring forever.
What happened once upon a time happens all the time.[15]

It is the *story* of the Exodus that matters, and our ability to find ourselves within that story even now, wherever and whenever we are. I am a woman in whom the past endures. I am a woman whose Promised Land lies before me. And, if I reach it, as I know I can, it will be as a person with all my creaturely limitations intact; it will be as a person who travels in the company of demons as well as angels; it will be as a person who has heard the voice of God.

Recovery from schizophrenia means any number of things to the people who pursue it. For some, it means the complete eradication of psychotic symptoms. And while I take great comfort in the periods of respite my medications offer from the psychotic experiences that come with an illness like mine, recovery, for me, means more than the mere absence of psychosis. It means building a life that includes psychosis but is worth living all the same. It means staying alive, yes. But more than that, it means seeking the Promised Land with all the companions who have journeyed with me from Egypt.

That is easier said than done, of course, but killing the devil has never been an option for me. Far be it from me to become complicit in the destruction of this old friend, after all.

Eleven

A Past for Adam

ON 29 AUGUST 2017, a coalition of evangelical Christians affiliated with the "Council for Biblical Manhood and Womanhood" ("CBMW") published the "Nashville Statement." It was a series of fourteen affirmations and denials offered "in the hope of serving Christ's church and witnessing publicly to the good purposes of God for human sexuality revealed in Christian Scripture."[1] Sex is to be restricted to monogamous, heterosexual marriages, the Statement declared, for it is "sin" that "distorts sexual desires by directing them away from the marriage covenant and toward sexual immorality."[2]

Although they censured heterosexual immorality as well, the Statement's authors reserved the lion's share of their condemnations for homosexual and transgender persons who refuse to adopt gender essentialist self-conceptions and submit to a life of voluntary chastity (or enforced heterosexuality). Article 10, which anathematizes Christian 2SLGBTQ+ persons and their allies, is illustrative:

> WE AFFIRM that it is sinful to approve of homosexual im-
> morality or transgenderism and that such approval constitutes
> an essential departure from Christian faithfulness and witness.

WE DENY that the approval of homosexual immorality or transgenderism is a matter of moral indifference about which otherwise faithful Christians should agree to disagree.[3]

Unsurprisingly, the Statement's release ignited a firestorm of controversy. Commentators and Christian activists denounced it in counter-polemics that variously compared the Statement to past Christian efforts to provide theological justifications for antisemitism, apartheid, and slavery.[4] And, of course, the counter-polemics were right. Their urgent tone spoke to the particular damage that the Nashville Statement's homophobic and transphobic rhetoric inflicted on those who found themselves objects of the censures therein yet nevertheless wished to continue identifying as evangelicals.

The Nashville Statement was harmful, even violent; and illuminated with particular clarity mainstream evangelicalism's complicity with ascendant anti-queer politics in Canada and the United States. But does that mean the Nashville Statement must be destroyed in its entirety?

It is a question that fascinates me because, while I want to say *yes*, I know that following through on that yes is an impossibility. The Nashville Statement—along with every other statement Christians have made denouncing people like myself—will always be out there; it can never be taken back or undone. You can burn books, or, in this case, published statements; but not ideas.

The impulse to throw the Nashville Statement into the fire fascinates me for another reason, too. Evangelical queerphobia is the contemporary culmination of a long theological tradition. The Nashville Statement did not come from nowhere; it is grounded in other texts, most notably the Bible.

A quotation from Psalm 100:3 introduces the Nashville Statement itself, and a litany of Scripture citations were included in a post-publication draft of the document. However, while the authors of the Nashville Statement framed their declaration as an articulation of fundamental scriptural teachings, one would be hard-pressed to find an evangelical critic who holds that, in order to defeat the Statement, Christian communities must jettison the Bible itself. More typical is the strategy adopted by the framers of the "Christians United Statement" (issued a day after the publication of the Nashville Statement), who portrayed their acceptance of 2SLGBTQ+ persons as a recovery of, rather than a departure from, key teachings in Scripture and the Christian tradition.[5]

But might other texts be suitable only for the flames?

If you are committed to burning the Nashville Statement, it would not be too much of a stretch to think that you should likewise take a torch to the writings of the Statement's initial (and perhaps subsequent) signatories. For if these persons were able, given their personal theological commitments, to subscribe publicly to the Nashville Statement, would this not suggest that their other contributions to the Christian theological archive are antithetical to queer flourishing?

And thus do we stand on the precipice of a treacherous slippery slope. Take evangelical-Anglican theologian J.I. Packer's written works, which would be strong candidates for incineration regardless of their author's endorsement of the Nashville Statement given Packer's repeated insistence that the inclusion of 2SLGBTQ+ persons within the church represents a deviation from Christian orthodoxy.[6] Asked during an interview for the highly conservative website *The Gospel Coalition* to enumerate the books that have had the greatest impact on his life, Packer put John Calvin's *The Institutes of the Christian Religion* at the "head of the list."[7] In so doing he established a bibliographic connection between his own writings (of which the Nashville Statement is one) and those of the sixteenth-century Protestant reformer. Want to understand Packer? You'll need to understand Calvin.

Now, the historical Calvin would be deeply confused by the modern and postmodern debates over human sexuality in which Packer is involved.[8] But if you take Packer's assessment of the *Institutes* at face value and see it as a formative (perhaps even defining) influence on Packer's thought, it is difficult to shake the feeling that the *Institutes* itself is in some way implicated in Packer's queerphobia. At the very least, Calvin's text might well be charged with guilt by association, and, on that basis, rejected as contrary to queer forms of Christian theology and practice.

By grounding his thought in Calvin's own, Packer turns the *Institutes* into the intellectual foundation for contemporary theological arguments that disempower and marginalize queer persons within Packer's evangelical community. To the extent that its content allows itself to be used in this way, the *Institutes* provides another reminder that the intellectual archive of Christian theological reflection in the West is hardly favourable (and, indeed, might well be openly hostile) to queer subjects. Rightly distressed by Packer's writings, queer evangelicals can be forgiven for viewing Calvin's text with suspicion, and regarding it as at least *potentially* a source of harm.

So what are such persons to do with the *Institutes*?

Interpret it.

How to Do Things with Texts

Interpretation is as much an act and an affective disposition as it is a discourse: What one does *to* and *with* a text is at least as significant as what one actually says *about* that text, if not more so.

To do something *with* a text, you need what I like to call an interpretive "script" for reading it. That is nothing other than a way of making sense of it. Language, by itself, is meaningless—pen strokes on a page only take the shape of letters and words because we have systems in place that allow us to see those strokes as communicative of meaning. Those systems are the languages we speak, and here I don't just mean English.

We all carry with us certain assumptions about *how* and *what* texts communicate to us. For example, if you are an evangelical who thinks that every word in the Bible is the capital-W Word of God, you probably also think that some readings of the Bible are "off-limits." For example, you probably don't think that it is appropriate to use the Song of Songs as a handbook for having kinky sex, even though some biblical scholars have suggested it can be read that way.[9] But you probably *do* think that the Bible contains meanings with personal and direct significance for your life, for example, instructions for how to establish a saving relationship with Jesus Christ.

To get technical for a minute, we can say that "interpretive scripts" are clusters of routinized strategies for doing things to/with texts that circumscribe domains of interpretive intelligibility.[10] Which is just a fancy way of pointing out that every community of people has its own ways of making words mean things. And that being a part of an interpretive community means using that community's scripts to interpret that community's texts in a way that makes sense to other people in that group. Don't show up to your Sunday book club quoting Jacques Derrida on deconstruction, even if both your book club and your graduate level seminar in English literature are reading the same classic text. And don't show up to your university seminar telling people that *The Picture of Dorian Gray* reminds you of the color blue. You won't make any sense. The interpretive script is so different, you might as well be speaking a different language.

If you're part of an interpretive community—and we are all part of a great many interpretive communities at any given time—there will already be scripts in place to guide your readings of that community's canonical texts, be they novels or the Bible. You don't need to reinvent the wheel. And, indeed, attempting to do so may lead to your exclusion.

That's because, in order to pass as an interpreter of your community's texts, you need to read those texts in a way that makes sense to other community members. Diverge a little from accepted reading practices, and people will say you're being idiosyncratic. Diverge a lot and people will start to doubt whether your interpretations make any sense. Diverge too much and people will not just say you're making things up; worse, they'll accuse you of committing violence against the texts in question.

Hence, amongst those for whom it is self-evident that fidelity to the biblical text requires the exclusion of 2SLGBTQ+ persons from the small-c catholic church, any effort to reconcile the inclusion of 2SLGBTQ+ persons within the church with the biblical witness to (for example) divine love are not merely wrong. They are certainly that. But, more importantly, such efforts are incomprehensible as ways of interpreting the Bible, perhaps even heretical attacks on the Bible itself.

All of which means two things.

First, there is very little difference between an interpretation of a text and the text itself. Texts only mean things because their readers *make* them mean things. And so, although we might distinguish between something like Calvin's *Institutes* and Packer's reading of that work for historical reasons, if you're in Packer's interpretive community the *Institutes* just is its queer-phobic interpretations. And this is because, if you want to stay in that community, you need to maintain some through line between your own readings of the *Institutes* (or the Bible, or whatever else that community thinks of as canonical) and the ones you consider harmful. Rejecting a canonical text is a surefire way to have your community reject you, after all.

Which brings me to my second point. To remain in community with people whose interpretive acts have harmed you, you have an obligation to in some way take ownership for those interpretive acts themselves, and not just the texts they are trying to make sense of. As a queer Christian, you occupy a precarious position. Insofar as you are Christian, you have to use your community's interpretive scripts even though those same scripts are seemingly incompatible with the actualization of queer identities. But insofar as you are queer nonetheless, you must engage in creative applications of those scripts in order to survive as who you are.

The question, then, is how to do that.

Of Heirs, Fanatics, and Canonical Texts

We're going to get abstract and technical for a few minutes, but bear with me.

Interpretive communities give their members texts as well as scripts for interpreting them. Some of these texts are canonical, in the sense that they are foundational to the community's self-understanding and must, consequently, be interpreted carefully if you are to remain a member of that group (think of the Bible). Some of these texts are proscribed, in the sense that they must *not* be interpreted using the group's interpretive scripts (for example, because they are "obscene"). And most texts are somewhere in between: you can read them however you like, without worrying about being marginalized or excluded because of your interpretations.

We are, all of us, *heirs* to our interpretive communities. Our interpretive heritage is both assigned and, through the acts of critical engagement and selective use that are necessary to keep that heritage alive, chosen.[11] Our heritage chooses us; but we also choose to inherit it.

Finitude—the fact of limitation—makes inheritance possible in the first place. The nothingness of death surrounds our existence; it is but a moment away. But that means we have the option to inherit that which transcends our finite existence, "receiv[ing] what is larger and older and more powerful than [us]. But the same finitude obliges [us] to choose, to prefer, to sacrifice, to exclude, to let go and leave behind. Precisely in order to respond to the call that preceded [us], to answer it and to answer for it – in [our] name as in the name of the other."[12]

The Infinite, God, cannot inherit because there is no thing that precedes God in time or exceeds the bounds of God's being. Inheritance necessarily involves choosing some things to preserve but not others, for the simple reason that we do not have time to preserve it all. The Infinite need make no such choice because it has, quite literally, all the time in the world.

Fanatics, likewise, do not inherit, albeit for different reasons. Rather than sifting through their inheritance to sort the gems from the dirt, they identify with it. And they do so in an effort to turn their inheritance into something that transcends finitude, which is to say, into God.[13] Gone is any sense that the tradition itself might be flawed, or that it might not have all of the answers. Gone is any motivation to answer for yourself. The fanatic is merely a vessel through which the evangelical tradition of reading the Bible speaks, to give just one example of fanaticism. And in the attempt to "preserve it all," the fanatic's self is lost.

When it comes to texts that have harmed you—like the Nashville State-ment or Calvin's *Institutes*—your only real option is to inherit them. The problem with such texts, you see, is that they can neither be abandoned nor ignored: Despite your best efforts to suppress them, they live on, making their presence known even after you have largely forgotten their contents.[14] This is true even if you are willing to renounce your membership in the communities in which those texts are canonical. Because you were formed in those communities, you cannot simply renounce their hold on your life; regardless of whatever other interpretive communities you might join, your identity will always have been constituted, at least in part, by the scripts that predominated in the communities you left. Hence it is impossible to ever truly be "ex-evangelical," for example.

If you are unwilling or unable to depart from your communities, how-ever, your indebtedness is all the more pronounced—and onerous. Since fanatical identification with those communities' traditions would foreclose the possibility of challenging their canons in order to renew those texts as something other than a cause of suffering, you must instead take up the role of an inheritor. However, in choosing to give new life to those traditions you as the heir are obliged to take responsibility for your community's history of violence. For, even though you have been a victim of that violence, it is still an element of the heritage that has chosen you.

Okay. Enough with the abstraction and the theory. Let's get very practical: Should queer evangelicals simply burn Calvin's *Institutes* along with Packer's writings?

Packer imagined himself to be an heir of Calvin's text; recall the interview he gave to *The Gospel Coalition*. And while the *Institutes* itself did not orig-inally speak to modern questions of human sexuality, Packer's interpretive acts—his support for the Nashville Statement not least—have given this text a future quite unlike the one Calvin could have imagined for his work.

If you can't leave Packer's evangelical community behind—not really, not ever—could you become an inheritor of that community's texts, too?

I think so. In fact, I think you have to.

Saving Calvin's *Institutes* from the Flames

Writing in an article for *The Gospel Coalition*, celebrity evangelical pastor Timothy Keller reflected on his experience of reading Calvin's *Institutes* in its entirety over the course of a single calendar year.[15] Having previously "treated the [*Institutes*] like an encyclopedia or dictionary that one dipped into to learn about specific topics," and conscious of Calvin's caricatured "reputation as a pinched, narrow-minded, cold, and cerebral dogmatician," Keller was pleasantly surprised to discover that not only are the contents of the *Institutes* thoroughly grounded in the words of Scripture, but the text as a whole is markedly "doxological:" "Calvin's writings don't read at all like a theological treatise, but like a man's meditating on the Scripture before God. The language is filled with reverence and awe, and often tenderness. That means that, despite the close reasoning of so many parts of the material, Calvin was all about the heart."[16]

Keller himself was not a signatory of the Nashville Statement, but his views on human sexuality are consistent with it. The Bible prohibits homosexuality, he has argued, not because its authors were "motivated by animosity toward people with same sex attraction," but, rather, "because homosexual practice doesn't fit with God's wonderful purposeful design for sexuality in our lives."[17] That design has three components. First, sex is a means of achieving "whole *life covenant bonding*" between two persons and, consequently, is appropriate only within the institution of marriage. Second, since that bonding is intended to reunite "complementary but separate genders," it is to be further restricted to marital unions between male and female persons. And, finally, within these heterosexual relationships sex is to serve a procreative function.[18]

Now, you are probably thinking that I have brought up Keller's overtly heterosexist views in conjunction with his admittedly moving meditation on the *Institutes* to raise doubts about Calvin's text being anything other than a dangerous one for queer evangelicals. But, to the contrary, I actually want to enlist Keller as an unlikely ally in my efforts to save the *Institutes* from the flames. For however tempting it may be to suggest that those harmed by Calvin's text should simply discard it, that strategy is untenable for those whose identities—as evangelicals, as interpreters—are based on the canonicity of the *Institutes*.

In order to flourish, these people—and I have to include myself amongst them—are better served by opening ourselves *à la* Keller to the possibility of being surprised by Calvin's text, for better and for worse. This is a treacherous course to plot, to be sure, but it is fortunately one that benefits from resources within the *Institutes* itself. The *Institutes* might always be dangerous (and not only for queer readers); yet, as historian Bruce Gordon rightly reminds us, one of the book's principal strengths remains its inexhaustible ability to "defy expectations, even among those unwilling to accept its conclusions."[19]

What I want to do is take Calvin's description of "piety" and use it to construct an interpretive strategy for reading not only the *Institutes* itself but canonical texts in general.

For Calvin, piety is closely linked to the knowledge of God. Knowing God means apprehending God's "powers" (including wisdom and truth) by witnessing God's works in creation,[20] not penetrating the depths of God's essence.[21] While such knowledge, which follows initially from an awareness that God created and sustains the universe, inevitably leads people to ascribe some reverence to the Divine, Calvin is insistent that "it will not suffice simply to hold that there is One whom all ought to honor and adore unless we are also persuaded that he is the fountain of every good, and that we must seek nothing elsewhere than in him."[22] Knowing God in this second sense means "tast[ing] his fatherly love,"[23] that is, apprehending Divinity as the source and cause of all wisdom, righteousness, and truth and responding in the only possible way: with gratitude as we "love and worship [God] in return."[24]

Piety, then, is "that reverence joined with love of God which the knowledge of his benefits induces."[25] This is less a matter of belief than an affective disposition towards the Father God;[26] piety gives rise to "pure and real religion," because in coming to know God, people learn "to seek every good from

148

him, and, having received it, to credit it to his account" through worship, obedience, and prayer.[27]

Calvin's account of piety in the *Institutes* enacts the very sense of awe that the reformer seeks to evoke in his readers vis-à-vis Divinity. As theologian Serene Jones puts it, Calvin adopts the "doxological voice,"[28] using first-person plural pronouns to transform his readers from passive observers into active participants in his own rhetorical performance of the reverence he is trying to inspire: God "nourishes *us* by his power, governs *us* by his providence, nourishes *us* by his goodness, and attends *us* with all sorts of blessings," and it is "we" who, by fixing our sights upon God's providential care, may thereby "learn to await and seek all these things from him."[29]

It is with a spirit of trust and gratitude analogous to that which characterizes the pious mind that, I think, interpreters should engage harmful canonical texts. Now texts, unlike God, are finite and, therefore, are never unambiguous sources of goodness.[30] But the converse also holds true, namely, that the ambiguity of texts is such that they are never so entirely evil as to be devoid of the potential to work good.[31] A pious interpreter takes advantage of this ambiguity, and repeatedly turns to her community's canonical texts as foundational elements of her own identity despite the damage those texts have caused. She is obligated to do so, for she is who and what she is because she was chosen by this heritage; to paraphrase Calvin, she owes her life to it.[32] Far from being naïve (in Ricoeur's first sense) about these texts' capacity to cause destruction, however, the posture of interpretive piety she adopts is grounded in the knowledge (derived from personal experience) that those texts have wounded her (and others) in the past and are likely to do so again in the future.

Yet, the pious interpreter desires those texts to contribute to her own growth and healing by speaking in unforeseen and, perhaps, ultimately cathartic ways. This desire translates into what Sedgwick terms "a reparative impulse" in which, fearing "that the culture surrounding [her] is inadequate or inimical to [her] nurture," the interpreter "wants to assemble and confer plenitude on an object that will then have resources to offer to an inchoate self."[33] That is to say, the reparative interpreter neither permits her past interactions with her community's foundational texts to determine future ones, nor insists that past interactions that were violent or destructive were exclusively so. Directing her interpretive energies towards her heritage in the belief that it can yet contribute to her own unending process of becoming, the reparative (like the pious) reader adopts a posture of hope.

Hope not only "that the future may be different from the present," but also that "the past, in turn, could have happened differently from the way it did."[34]

Another word for that hope is gratitude. Thankful for the influence of a community's canonical texts and interpretive scripts on her own formation as a self, the pious interpreter commits herself to inheriting those traditions, optimistic that they have yet more to contribute to who she is. For, however much said traditions have wounded her, she cannot imagine her life except as a member of her community and an interpreter of its canon. Out of love for her heritage, she consequently works to heal (or repair) that community's traditions in order that those traditions might be a source of healing for herself. It is this "future-to-come" that the pious queer interpreter of the *Institutes* not only dares to dream but endeavors to actualize,[35] a project that requires her to begin, like Keller, by reading Calvin's text and finding herself surprised.

So What Do We Do with the Nashville Statement?

It is probably a bit of an overstatement to characterize either Packer's writings or the Nashville Statement as canonical in the way I have been using that term. Although it could perhaps be said that, within conservative evangelical circles, they fall closer to the canonical end of the interpretive spectrum than to the proscribed/obscene one. Nonetheless, what I have said about interpreting canonical texts still applies.

You cannot free yourself entirely from these texts. Nor should you want to. Remember, you are who you are because of the community that raised you, with all its hatred and bigotries and harm.

But once the limits of liberation are recognized, opportunities emerge for queer evangelicals to engage in an innovative and nuanced sort of coalitional politics.[36] Refusing to renounce their claims to being both queer *and* evangelical, such persons can, instead, re-negotiate the content of these terms. "Queer evangelical" is a sufficiently capacious phrase to include those people who self-identify as such while also capturing the views of those who, like Packer, equate evangelical Christianity with reactionary views on gender and sexuality.

For discourses that oppress need not necessarily do so. Harmful texts are not only destructive. And queer people have the opportunity, *as heirs*, to take up both Packer's corpus and the Nashville Statement as allies in the cause of articulating who they are *as evangelicals*.

I am suggesting a practice of critical reception that denies both Packer and the other framers of the Nashville Statement the last word on the meaning and import of their respective contributions to the evangelical heritage. A practice that thereby asserts the authority of queer evangelicals as creative contributors to the evangelical tradition.

Might Calvin's *Institutes* guide that practice? I think so.

The prefatory remarks that frame the Nashville Statement's affirmations and denials provide some clues on this front. In these, the Statement's framers both acknowledge that God—*qua* the "Creator and Lord of all"— is the one to whom "every person owes glad-hearted thanksgiving, heart-felt praise, and total allegiance," and subsequently confess their belief that God's providential governance of the cosmos "bring[s] us the greatest good."[37] These are the same sorts of comments that, in Calvin's *Institutes*, the pious mind makes when it apprehends the Divine. A reparative intervention into the Nashville Statement done in the light of the reparative reading of Calvin I undertook in this chapter might begin, therefore, by accepting these elements of the Statement's construal of God, wagering on the possibility that they allude also to the Statement's relationship with its evangelical readership, and thereby finding some grounds for optimism. From there it would remain—as was the case with the *Institutes* itself—for interpreters to make good on that hope: tracking the trajectory of this Nashville-piety as it unfolds—somewhat ironically, perhaps—across the subsequent rhetoric, but without predetermining, for good or for ill, the outcome of doing so.

Interpretation as a Way of Life

I hesitate to criticize those who would simply do away with texts and interpretive strategies that have been the causes of trauma. However, I cannot subscribe to a course of action that would respond to destruction with yet more violence. To do so might be a way to die, but it is no way to live. If interpretation is as much a matter of how you conduct yourself as of what you say, an interpreter who works to obliterate a text has adopted a troubling interpretive strategy indeed.

I for one prefer love, hope, and gratitude over anger, suspicion, and vengeance. For I am an heir to the Christian communities that have hurt me. And that means allowing those communities' texts to speak in unexpected, unintended, and perhaps even unsettling ways in order that they might become sources of life.

PART SIX
Life, Interrupted

My first note was long and eloquent.

I wanted to say everything. That I was a ship lost at sea, unable to remain upright against the crashing waves any longer. That not everyone can recover, and it's no one's fault I couldn't recover, either. That I would like to rest, in the end, along the banks of the Milk River within view of the Sweetgrass Hills: as far as I'm concerned, the most beautiful place on earth.

My second note read much the same.

It's amazing to me how something so personal so quickly becomes a recitation of personal clichés. I didn't have to labour over this note: I'd written it before.

I don't remember my third note. Or my fourth. Or how many notes there have been these past years, the words the same every time. Writing them has become something of a chore I reserve for my darkest days, and chores have a tendency to blur together in the mind.

The other day, I sat down to write another note. Only, this time, I had nothing to say beyond a generic apology. I tried to recite lines I'd written previously, but they carried no weight; they meant nothing to me and I couldn't imagine them being my last words to the living.

The Talmud teaches that "'Whoever saves a single life is considered by scripture to have saved the whole world.' Because we are created in God's image." I have to believe that this applies not only to others but to ourselves, too. That each time I am on the brink of death, I am on the brink of destroying a whole world—and each time I pull myself back, it is a whole world I have saved.

I've never had to use my notes. I've always destroyed them before they could be read.

But for all their macabre quality, I have to wonder if writing them hasn't been its own way of working my way towards recovery.

There are words that can only be written during the darkest nights of the soul, when writing them is its own way of raging against the dying of the light. But perhaps the fact that I can't write them anymore means that the darkest nights have passed.

The dawn has broken through on a world no longer on the cusp of oblivion.

Twelve

UNTIL AT DAWN WE WAKE

THERE'S AN ABUSE CRISIS in North America's progressive denominations, and it's unfolding largely outside of the public eye.

Take my former denomination, The Episcopal Church.

Buried deep in the 2022 Reports to General Convention were the results of a survey, conducted in 2020, that quantifies the violence epidemic in that branch of the global Anglican Communion.[1] Based on a similar survey conducted in 2017 amongst United Methodists in the United States,[2] it contributes to the "truth telling" element of a planned truth-and-reconciliation process on gender and sexual abuse in Episcopal spaces.

And the truth is horrifying.

Of the more than 2400 responses collected, 475 (20 percent) are from cisgender LGB Episcopalians. Nearly 40 percent of these—189 individuals—reported being the targets of inappropriate jokes and comments; 29.9 percent—82 individuals—of inappropriate touching; and a further 14.9 percent—71 individuals—of attempted fondling or kissing.

The survey also uncovered alarming rates of attempted assault, including attempted rape. Among cisgender LGB respondents, 5.3 percent—25 individuals—disclosed being the targets of such misconduct, as compared to 2.4 percent of cisgender heterosexual respondents (a further 44 victims). The survey doesn't break down the data on completed sexual assaults or rapes by victims' sexual orientation. But in total, a staggering 3.5 percent of all respondents—86 individuals—identified themselves as being the victims of such violence in an Episcopal church (47 individuals), school (22 individuals), or workplace (17 individuals).

The percentages are even more striking when looking at the data for trans and nonbinary respondents.

Nearly 75 percent of Episcopal clergy who identify as such reported being the victims of sexual misconduct of some kind, as did 100 percent of those employed in non-ordained roles and 50 percent of congregation members.

The survey also found that trans and nonbinary respondents were victimized at higher rates than their cisgender counterparts across a range of inappropriate behaviours. To cite just one example: 39 percent disclosed inappropriate touching or closeness, compared to 27.2 percent of cisgender women and 16.4 percent of cisgender men.

The survey organizers caution that the data they collected is unlikely to be representative of Episcopalians as a whole. "Because victims/survivors are more likely to complete a survey on [their victimization]," they argue in the preface to their report, the percentage of respondents reporting gender and sexual violence "is surely higher than it would be if all Episcopalians had participated."

And to be sure, the data isn't based on a random sample size and therefore isn't statistically representative.

The number of individuals reporting victimization in Episcopal spaces is alarming, nonetheless.

However, I would argue the data is more likely to under- than to overestimate the scope of the abuse that occurs. To see why, the survey results must be interpreted in light of The Episcopal Church's larger culture of inaction around sexual violence.

See No Evil, Hear No Evil...

2SLGBTQ+ Episcopalians, and especially those who identify under the transgender and nonbinary umbrella, were far more likely than their cisgender and heterosexual counterparts to cite a fear that nothing would be done or that they'd be retaliated against as their top reasons *not* to report instances of sexual abuse to denominational authorities.

Those fears are, unfortunately, well-founded.

Of those victims who *did* report their victimization to Episcopal leaders, the number one assessment from both trans/nonbinary and cisgender respondents was that "little or no change" came about as a result. 20.6 percent of trans and nonbinary survivors reported that they simply left the church altogether. By comparison, "only" 10.7 percent of cisgender women felt they had to leave. (Curiously, there's no data on this front for LGB-identified Episcopalians.)

It would be difficult to come to any conclusion other than that the culture of The Episcopal Church is one in which "problem" victims who speak out are either ignored or made to go away. It's a wonder any abuse survivors responded to the denomination's survey at all.

The Dark Side of Inclusive Christianity

The data the survey nonetheless yielded would be sobering in any context. But it's a particularly striking look at on-the-ground realities in Episcopal churches because the denomination rests so much of its brand identity on being a safe haven for gender and sexual refugees from more conservative traditions.

"We have a legacy of inclusion," the denomination's website proudly states; a legacy that began with The Episcopal Church's General Convention formally affirming, in 1976, that "homosexual persons are children of God who have a full and equal claim with all other persons upon the love, acceptance, and pastoral concern and care of the Church."[3]

Indeed, in 2004, the denomination became the first in the Anglican Communion to consecrate an openly gay bishop, Gene Robinson. In 2021, however, Bishop Robinson inexplicably told LGBTQ+ Episcopalians, incensed that the denomination had invited noted-homophobe Max Lucado to preach from the Episcopal-run National Cathedral,[4] that "we've won."[5]

A month later, The Episcopal Church responded to a Vatican decree prohibiting Roman Catholic priests from blessing same-sex unions by tweeting "The Episcopal Church Welcomes You."[6] The tweet was deleted within an hour following a backlash from Twitter users who pointed out that there are still parts of the denomination that do not, in fact, welcome 2SLGBTQ+ members.[7]

Marketing itself (however flat-footedly) as the progressive, welcoming face of American Christianity makes sense as a way of distinguishing The Episcopal Church on the religious landscape from the evangelical Right and its culture wars against gay marriage and transgender rights, among other conservative bugaboos. Disaffected with the latter? The Episcopal Church welcomes you.

Here's the problem. This brand image is at odds with the fact that 2SLGBTQ+ Episcopalians experience sexual victimization in Episcopal spaces at consistently higher rates than their cisgender and heterosexual counterparts. So in order to preserve that image, reports of abuse need to go away—preferably quietly.

The result is a culture of silence in which survivors aren't heard, their stories aren't acted upon, and abusers remain in positions of power to abuse again. The sort of meaningful change that would actually protect 2SLGBTQ+ Episcopalians never occurs because that would mean acknowledging, publicly, that The Episcopal Church has a *systemic abuse crisis* in the first place.

The denomination can say what it likes about being a bastion of inclusivity. The fact is, it's not safe for 2SLGBTQ+ people.[8] And that's a theological problem.

Theology after Abuse

Because here's the thing about Christian baptism, the great rite of initiation into Christian community: It's irreversible.

Once baptized, "Everything old has passed away; ... everything has become new" (2 Corinthians 5:17 NRSV). No going back. As The Episcopal Church's baptismal liturgy puts it: you have been "marked as Christ's own forever."

Some—perhaps even most—baptized Christians might find the sacrament's irreversibility reassuring, a source of hope during the darkest hours of the night. Nothing they do, nothing done to them, will ever separate them from Christ, into whose death and resurrection they were baptized. Nor will anything separate them from Christ's body—the Church universal—of which the baptized are individual members.

But speaking as someone who was forced out of my own Episcopal church community through clerical misconduct, I just find it really frustrating.

More than once, I have prayed that God would find it in the unfathomable depths of divine mercy to erase this indelible mark on my soul; to free me from my new life in Christ; to break the Church's claim to me and my life. And every time to no avail. Like it or not, it seems, I will be born again until the day I die.

And I don't like it one bit. For my baptism has become a chain around my neck, binding me forever to my priest abuser. Hardly something to celebrate.

———————

Every baptism is a contract that imposes obligations and confers benefits on the three parties to it: God, the baptized, and the catholic Church.

Through their "Prayers for the Candidates," Episcopalians secure God's pledge, among other things, to renew the baptized in the resurrection life of God's Son and to bestow upon them the power of God's Holy Spirit. In return for these gifts, God receives the praise, obedience, and trust of God's people.

The baptized promise, among other things, to "renounce all sinful desires that draw [them] from the love of God" and to accept Christ Jesus as their savior. In exchange, the salvation God's Son secured becomes theirs by right, as does that special vehicle of divine grace God has made available to God's Church: the Holy Eucharist. Having gained a share in what the liturgy describes as Christ's "eternal priesthood," the baptized may—this time in the words of the Letter to the Hebrews—"approach the throne of grace with boldness."

What of the Church? It increases in size and ability to discharge its evangelistic mission to "make disciples of all nations" (Matthew 28:16–20). For that, the Church's local representatives—that is, the clergy and congregation present at an individual baptism—renew their own baptismal covenants with God. And, no less importantly, they make a pledge to the baptized themselves to, with God's help, "do all in [their] power to support [the baptized] in their life in Christ."

As is the case with any contract, the parties to a baptism may breach their commitments—and thereby become liable to the relevant consequences.

Through apostasy and excommunication, for example, the baptized forfeit certain of their sacramental rights.

If baptism is conversion, apostasy is its antonym: the experience of de-converting or falling away from the Christian faith. And if Hebrews 6:1–8 is to be believed, post-baptismal apostasy is just as irreversible.

"For it is impossible," the author of that book writes, "to restore again to repentance those who have once been enlightened, and have tasted the heavenly gift, and have shared in the Holy Spirit ... and then have fallen away, since on their own they are crucifying again the Son of God and holding him up to contempt."

The "enlightenment" in view here is the faith in Christ Jesus and repentance from sin that precedes and, indeed, motivates a person to undergo baptism (see vv. 1–2). Faith being a gift from God, it is "impossible" for apostates to be restored to enlightenment because God refuses to dispense that gift a second time to a person who received it once only to subsequently throw it away.

Why? Because these apostates have experienced crucifixion with Christ and yet have chosen to crucify Christ. Their reasons for doing so are irrelevant: what matters is that they have decisively severed their relationship with God's Son, and that God honors this expression of human agency by declining to undo their choice.

Like irrigated earth that produces only weeds, apostates experience the blessings of divine grace but later backslide into an unrepentant state. In so doing, they lose the guarantee of Christian salvation; their "end is to be burned" in the divine judgment against those who live in sin, no matter what they might later do.

It is possible, by contrast, to remedy one's excommunication from The Episcopal Church.

The *Book of Common Prayer*'s "Disciplinary Rubrics" contemplate four circumstances in which individual believers might exist in a state of impaired relationship with the larger Christian community. There are those occasions in which a person "is living a notoriously evil life [and] intends" to partake of the Eucharist. Those in which a person has wronged their neighbor and thereby become "a scandal to other members of the congregation." Those in which "there is hatred between members of the congregation." And, finally, those in which one of the parties to a dispute declines to forgive the other.

In all such cases, where the situation becomes known to the parish priest, that priest is to speak to the person(s) in question and advise them that they may not partake of the Eucharist until they have repented of their wrongs—including, where necessary, by making restitution to those they have harmed. Having done so, the priest is then to promptly notify their bishop as to their "reasons for refusing Communion."

While at first glance an act of cruelty, this informal rite of exclusion is perhaps better understood as an expression of Christian mercy. The express purpose behind it is to encourage what the prayer book terms "repentance and amendment of life." Moreover, it protects wicked believers from receiving the Eucharist unworthily, which, as St. Paul warned the Corinthians, would amount to "eat[ing] and drink[ing] judgment against [themselves]" (see 1 Corinthians 11:27–31).

It is, in other words, for the ultimate benefit of those under their charge that Episcopal priests are tasked with denying to some that to which they would otherwise be entitled by virtue of their baptism: the body and blood of Christ.

If the baptized may, through their actions, lose the rights and benefits that accrue to them at their Christian initiation, surely this must also be the case for the catholic Church in those cases where it, too, breaches its baptismal duties.

And breach those duties it does when, to name just a few abuses, the Church drives away faithful believers through discriminatory and exclusionary policies; sexual, physical, or emotional violence; and practices, by leaders lay or ordained, that prey on the vulnerable.

The Church's most basic obligation to the baptized is to include them in its corporate life. Hence, immediately after the baptized are "sealed by the Holy Spirit in baptism," priest and congregation assure them that "We receive you into the household of God." Without that welcome, their baptism would be incomplete; it is not an optional component of the liturgy.

When priest and congregation renege on this initial assurance, the bonds between the Church and its abused members loosen. Their relationship is impaired, no less than when baptized Christians renege on their own pledge to resist evil. The Church loses its claim to the abused—at least so long as it persists in an unreformed state, and maybe even eternally.

I am speculating at this point, of course; although not, I suspect, without some warrant.

God's presence is not confined to the Church, nor is God's justice and mercy. It is, rather, among the nations, whom God is also leading to salvation. "Did I not bring Israel up from the land of Egypt," God thus asks through the prophet Amos, "and the Philistines from Caphtor and the Arameans from Kir?" (Amos 9:7)

God's faithfulness to those the Church wounds and rejects is not in doubt, even if the Christian community's is. Perhaps, then, for such people baptism is not a chain that keeps us from escaping our abusers, but an anchor that keeps the abused from drifting too far from the knowledge of God's grace when the Church cuts us adrift.

It is an intangible and, indeed, indelible reminder that not a single thing "in all creation will be able to separate us from the love of God" (Romans 8:38–39). Not even Christians. Not even the Church. No matter where we might go. No matter where we might make our home.

Perhaps there is something hopeful about baptism's irreversibility, after all.

My Hope is in People

I don't know what God is above us or what devils below, but I know this: our home is among people. People, in all their frailty and finitude, who have a tenacious ability to thrive despite the worst adversity. People who have the power to create and to destroy, to build up and to tear down, to heal and to injure.

And it was among people that, as a seminarian with a felt call to the Anglican priesthood, I embarked on a ministry internship at an Episcopal church community. The abuse that followed began with my priest supervisor asking inappropriately personal questions about my transitioning body, was marked by him making inhospitable jokes about "men in dresses," and ended with him forcing me out of my ministry role for trying to establish professional boundaries. I was lucky that that was all his misconduct entailed.

That experience, and the lack of support I subsequently received from The Episcopal Church when I reported my priest supervisor's malfeasance, shattered my faith. In the years since, I have had to pick up the broken pieces. But I have not done so alone.

These days, my spiritual home is amongst Jews, in whose company I keep *Shabbat* and pursue holiness in every aspect of my life.

I will never leave Christianity behind entirely. I can't. It is, after all, my inheritance; and I am who I am because of how Christians raised and educated me.

I am no longer confessionally Christian, in an active or present sense. But I still have hope for Christians. For the Church is not eternal. It is finite, limited, and temporally bound. It is made up of people. People who can and do change: God-willing, eventually.

Follow Highway 2 north, past the sprawling suburbs and gaudy mega-malls. Take the northernmost off-ramp, onto Highway 547. Drive until the city gives way to the prairie. Then keep going.

If you have never before visited this land of endless sky, your disorientation will be acute.

You will see further than you ever have before. Far-distant objects will haunt the horizon, an impossible number of miles away. But in an instant, they will be upon you; and just as quickly, they will be no more than reflections in your rear-view mirror.

Trust the road, your guide and your salvation, and keep driving through it all.

Soon enough you'll arrive at a little country church—painted Puritan white; its tower penetrating the prairie sky, but still barely visible through the surrounding shelterbelt—that I've seen a handful of times with my eyes, and countless times with my mind.

It is a place that exists more in memory that in fact.

It is my safe place.

Now it can be yours, too.

For there, together as sailors on a sea of grass, we can watch the sun rise high over the eastern sky.

ENDNOTES

I, Ezekiel

1. As the present book is directed primarily at Christians, I generally use the Christian term "Old Testament" for what I have come to know as just the "Bible" or the "Hebrew Bible." For more on my own religious subject position in relation to this book, see Chapter Three: The Paths Ahead.

2. See, e.g., Daniel I Block, *The Book of Ezekiel: Chapters 1—24* (NICOT; Grand Rapids: Eerdmans, 1997), 154.

3. Edwin C. Broome, Jr., "Ezekiel's Abnormal Personality," *Journal of Biblical Literature* 65:3 (1946): 290.

4. A cis/cisgender person is someone whose gender identity lines up with their sex assigned at birth.

5. Paul Tillich, *Systematic Theology: Volume 1* (Chicago: University of Chicago Press, 2012), 13.

6. Ableism, in short, means lifting up the able-bodied (read: not disabled) while putting down anything that smacks of disability.

7. Kathryn Tanner, *Jesus, Humanity, and the Trinity: A Brief Systematic Theology* (Minneapolis: Fortress, 2001), 56.

DSM Dreams

1. "Gender Dysphoria in Adolescents and Adults" in *Diagnostic and Statistical Manual of Mental Disorders* (5th ed.; Arlington, VA: American Psychiatric Association, 2013), 452-453.

2. See e.g., Jeffrey A Lieberman, *Malady of the Mind: Schizophrenia and the Path to Prevention* (New York: Scribner, 2023), 122.

3. The best resource for learning about the hearing voices movement are the movements' various websites, for example, "About HVN," National Hearing Voices Network, accessed April 18, 2024, https://www.hearing-voices.org/about-us/.

4. Dirk Corstens, Eleanor Longden, Simon McCarthy-Jones, Rachel Waddingham & Neil Thomas, "Emerging Perspectives From the Hearing Voices Movement: Implications for Research and Practice," *Schizophrenia Bulletin* 40: Supplement 4 (2014): S285.

5. See "Welcome," National Hearing Voices Network, accessed April 18, 2024, https://www.hea ring-voices.org/.

6. See F. Waters, J. D. Blom, R. Jardri, K. Hugdahl & I. E. C. Sommer, "Auditory Hallucinations, Not Necessarily a Hallmark of Psychotic Disorder," *Psychological Medicine* 48:4 (2017).

7. See, similarly, Francine Russo, "Where Transgender is no Longer a Diagnosis," *Scientific American* (January 6, 2017), https://www.scientificamerican.com/article/where-transgender-is-no-l onger-a-diagnosis/.

8. Kaley Whalen, "(In)validating Transgender Identities: Progress and Trouble in the DSM-5," National LGBTQ Task Force, December 12, 2012, https://www.thetaskforce.org/news/inval idating-transgender-identities-progress-and-trouble-in-the-dsm-5/.

9. In the rest of the world, that would be an "Anglican" priest.

10. Esmé Weijun Wang, *The Collected Schizophrenias* (Minneapolis: Graywolf Press, 2019), 5.

Madness, Neurodivergence

1. See, e.g., Matthew D. Erlich et al., "Schizophrenia and Other Psychotic Disorders," in *Psychiatry*, by Janis L. Cutler, 3rd ed. (Oxford: Oxford University Press, 2014), 104; Elyn R. Saks, *The Center Cannot Hold: My Journey through Madness* (New York: Hachette Books, 2007), 328 and *passim*.

2. "As many as 30 to 50% of individuals with the disorder follow a progressive course with cumulative residual symptoms, which suggests that there may be a neuroprogressive component in addition to the neurodevelopmental one" (Ramiro Reckziegel et al., "Heterogeneous Trajectories in Schizophrenia: Insights from Neurodevelopment and Neuroprogression Models," *Braz J Psychiatry* 44, no. 1 (2022): 74–80.)

3. That's the thrust of the argument Jeffrey Lieberman makes in his monumental book on the illness, *Malady of the Mind: Schizophrenia and the Path to Prevention* (New York: Scribner, 2023).

4. See the *Oxford English Dictionary*, s.v. "prodrome (*adj.*)," September 2023, https://doi.org/10.1093/OED/3002963843.

5. So, e.g., Molly K Larson, Elaine F Walker & Michael T Compton, "Early Signs, Diagnosis and Therapeutics of the Prodromal Phase of Schizophrenia and Related Psychotic Disorder," *Expert Rev Neurother* 10:8 (2010).

6. Robert Menzies, Brenda A. LeFrançois, and Geoffrey Reaume, "Introducing Mad Studies," in *Mad Matters: A Critical Reader in Canadian Mad Studies*, ed. Brenda A. LeFrançois, Robert Menzies, and Geoffrey Reaume (Toronto: Canadian Scholars' Press, 2013), 10.

7. See Ellen van Wolde, "Separation and Creation in Genesis 1 and Psalm 104, A Continuation of the Discussion of the Verb [br']." *Vetus Testamentum* 67:4 (2017): 611-647.

8. Monique Botha et al., "The Neurodiversity Concept Was Developed Collectively: An Overdue Correction on the Origins of Neurodiversity Theory," *Autism*, 2024, https://doi.org/10.1177/13623613241237871.

9. So, e.g., Patrick Dwyer, "The Neurodiversity Approach(es): What Are They and What Do They Mean for Researchers?," *Human Development* 66, no. 2 (2022): 73–92, https://doi.org/10.1159/000523723 .

10. See, e.g., Erin Gregory, "What Does It Mean to Be Neurodivergent?," *Forbes*, February 20, 2024, https://www.forbes.com/health/mind/what-is-neurodivergent/.

11. See, e.g., "What Causes Psychosis?," *Early Psychosis Intervention*, May 16, 2019, https://www.earlypsychosis.ca/what-causes-psychosis/.

12. See Lieberman, *Malady of the Mind*, 139-141.

13. Ibid, 141.

14. See, e.g., Kara Gavin, "When Reality Fails: What to Know about Psychosis," Michigan Medicine, June 9, 2022, https://www.michiganmedicine.org/health-lab/when-reality-fails-what-know-about-psychosis.

15. Marcin Rzadeczka, Maciej Wodziński, and Marcin Moskalweicz, "Cognitive Biases as an Adaptive Strategy in Autism and Schizophrenia Spectrum: The Compensation Perspective on Neurodiversity," *Frontiers in Psychiatry* 14 (2023), https://doi.org/10.3389/fpsyt.2023.1291854.

16. J.M. Atkinson, "To Tell or Not to Tell the Diagnosis of Schizophrenia," *Journal of Medical Ethics* 15, no. 1 (1989): 166–67.

17. See, e.g., Elyn R. Saks, "Successful and Schizophrenic," *New York Times*, January 27, 2013, https://www.nytimes.com/2013/01/27/opinion/sunday/schizophrenic-not-stupid.html.

18. Elyn R. Saks, *The Center Cannot Hold: My Journey through Madness* (New York: Hachette Books, 2007), 288.

19. So, e.g., Nancy Levene, *Powers of Distinction: On Religion and Modernity* (Chicago: University of Chicago Press, 2017), 8: "Inclusion is a distinction, a distinction both from positions that distinguish invidiously and from those that do not distinguish at all. It is paradoxically distinction by which inclusion comes to be possible."

Disability and the Seventh Day

1. Abraham Joshua Heschel, *The Sabbath: Its Meaning for Modern Man* (New York: Farrar, Straus & Giroux, 1951), 8.

2. Ibid, 21.

3. Ibid.

4. Ibid.

5. Ibid, 3 (emphasis mine).

6. See Ecclesiastes 3:1-8.

7. Heschel, *The Sabbath*, 100.

8. Ibid.

9. Wendy Brown, *Undoing the Demos: Neoliberalism's Stealth Revolution* (Cambridge: The MIT Press, 2015), 31 (emphasis original).

10. Ibid, 33.

11. Heschel, *The Sabbath*, 28.

12. Ibid.

13. Ibid, 21.

14. "But to the Bible the idea of the good is penultimate; it cannot exist without the holy. The good is the base, the holy is the summit. Things created in six days He considered *good*, the seventh day He made *holy*" (Ibid, 75).

15. Ibid, 32. See Exodus 20:9-11.

16. See, e.g., Heschel, *The Sabbath*, 73.

17. Ibid, 74.

18. Ibid, 101.

19. See George Robinson, *Essential Judaism: A Complete Guide to Beliefs, Customs, and Rituals* (New York: Atria, 2016), 85-86.

20. See Benjamin L Berger, *Law's Religion: Religious Difference and the Claims of Constitutionalism* (Toronto: University of Toronto Press, 2015), 43.

21. *Rosenberg v Outremont (City)*, 2001 CanLII 25087 (QC SC), para 18.

22. Berger, *Law's Religion*, 119.

23. Ibid, 118-119.

24. 42 USC § 12101.

25. Kevin M Barry, "Disabilityqueer: Federal Disability Rights Protection for Transgender People," *Yale Human Rights and Development Law Journal* 16 (2013): 1.

26. See the *ADA*, sec 3(2).

27. See the *ADA*, sec 511(a).

28. See the *ADA*, sec 511(b).

29. Jasbir K. Puar, *The Right to Maim: Debility, Capacity, Disability*, Anima (Durham, NC: Duke University Press, 2017), 40.

30. Quoted in Barry, "Disabilityqueer," 13.

31. Ibid, 13.

32. See ibid, 14.

33. Ibid, 25.

34. Ibid, 50.

35. Ibid, 29.

36. Ibid.

37. Ibid, 42-43.

38. David Wasserman and Sean Aas, "Disability: Definitions and Models," in *The Stanford Encyclopedia of Philosophy*, ed. Edward N Zalta and Uri Nodelman, 2023, https://plato.stanford.edu/entries/disability/.

39. See, e.g., World Health Organization, *International Classification of Impairment, Disability and Handicap* (Geneva: World Health Organization, 1980).

40. Michael Oliver, "A New Model of the Social Work Role in Relation to Disability," in *The Handicapped Person: A New Perspective for Social Workers*, ed. J Campling (London: RADAR, 1981), 19–32.

41. See, e.g., Sarah Buder and Rose Perry, "The Social Model of Disability Explained," *Social Creatures*, April 12, 2023, https://www.thesocialcreatures.org/thecreaturetimes/the-social-model-of-disability; Benjamin Reiss, David Serlin, and Rachel Adams, "Disability," in *Keywords for Disability Studies*, ed. Rachel Adams, Benjamin Reiss, and David Serlin (New York: New York University Press, 2015).

42. Puar, *The Right to Maim*, xv.

43. Heschel, *The Sabbath*, 28.

44. Ibid, 28.

45. Ibid, 30.

46. Puar, *The Right to Maim*, xvi.

47. See Leviticus 19:3.

48. Nancy L Eiesland, *The Disabled God: Toward a Liberatory Theology of Disability* (Nashville: Abingdon, 1994), 103.

49. See Ezekiel 10:18 and surrounding.

50. I am informed here by, e.g., John Swain and Sally French, "Towards an Affirmative Model of Disability," *Disability & Society* 15, no. 4 (2000): 569–82.

The Valley of the Shadow of Death

1. "Correctional Service Canada Finally Releases Video Footage of Guards' Excessive Force against a Person in Prison," *PLS: Prisoners' Legal Services*, May 9, 2023, https://prisonjustice.org/news-release-correctional-service-canada-finally-releases-video-footage-of-guards-excessive-force-against-a-person-in-prison/; Denico Lourenco, "Newly-Released Footage Shows Guards' Excessive Force against Indigenous Prisoner," *CTV News*, May 16, 2023, https://www.ctvnews.ca/canada/newly-released-footage-shows-guards-excessive-force-against-indigenous-prisoner-1.6400731.

2. In Canada, there are provincial as well as federal carceral institutions. The former are prisons, the latter are penitentiaries. People sentenced to carceral sentences of two years or longer are housed in federal institutions. They are my focus in this chapter.

3. Shanna Farrell MacDonald et al., "Examination of Gender Diverse Offenders" (Ottawa: Correctional Service of Canada, 2022).

4. The amending bill was Bill C-16, *An Act to amend the Canadian Human Rights Act and the Criminal Code*, 1st Sess, 42nd Parl, 2015-2016-2017 (assented to June 19, 2017).

5. *Commissioner's Directive 100: Gender Diverse Offenders* (Ottawa: Correctional Service Canada, 2022), https://www.canada.ca/en/correctional-service/corporate/acts-regulations-policy/commissioners-directives/100.html.

6. See Randall Garrison, "White Paper on the Status of Trans and Gender Diverse People," June 2013, https://randallgarrison.ndp.ca/sites/default/files/white_paper_on_the_status_of_trans_and_gender_diverse_people-_english__0.pdf, 13.

7. See Charlotte Dalwood, "Wait Times for Bottom Surgery in Canada Can Be As Long as Eight Years. The Impact on Individuals Can Be Deadly," *Xtra Magazine*, August 16, 2023, https://xtramagazine.com/health/wait-times-trans-bottom-surgery-canada-255804.

8. 2019 FC 456.

9. See Denico Lourenco, "Indigenous Trans Woman Seeks Changes over 'Unnecessarily Degrading' Prison Policy," *Xtra Magazine*, April 14, 2023, https://xtramagazine.com/power/trans-prison-complaint-gender-marker-249099.

10. Part I of the *Constitution Act, 1982*, being Schedule B to the *Canada Act 1982* (UK), 1982, c 11, s 91(24).

11. See Janelle N. Beaudette and Lynn A. Stewart, "National Prevalence of Mental Disorders among Incoming Canadian Male Offenders," *Canadian Journal of Psychiatry* 61, no. 10 (2016): 624–32.

12. Ibid.

13. G.P. Brown et al., "Prevalence of Mental Disorder among Federally Sentenced Women Offenders: In-Custody and Intake Samples" (Ottawa: Correctional Service of Canada, 2018).

14. Ibid.

15. Colin Cameron et al., "Psychiatry in the Federal Correctional System in Canada," *BJPsych International* 18, no. 2 (2021): 42–46.

16. Ibid.

17. See, e.g., "Ending Mass Incarceration," Vera Institute of Justice, accessed May 13, 2024, https://www.vera.org/ending-mass-incarceration.

18. "United States of America | World Prison Brief," accessed May 13, 2024, https://www.prisonstudies.org/country/united-states-america.

19. "Serious Mental Illness (SMI) Prevalence in Jails and Prisons" (Treatment Advocacy Center, 2016), https://www.treatmentadvocacycenter.org/reports_publications/serious-mental-illness-prevalence-in-jails-and-prisons/.

20. Ibid. See also the discussion in Stephanie Mencimer, "There Are 10 Times More Mentally Ill People Behind Bars than in State Hospitals," *Mother Jones*, April 8, 2014, https://www.motherjones.com/criminal-justice/2014/04/record-numbers-mentally-ill-prisons-and-jails/.

21. Megan J. Wolff, "Fact Sheet: Incarceration and Mental Health" (Weill Cornell Medicine, May 30, 2017), https://psychiatry.weill.cornell.edu/research-institutes/dewitt-wallace-institute-psychiatry/issues-mental-health-policy/fact-sheet-0.

22. Matt Ford, "America's Largest Mental Hospital Is a Jail," *The Atlantic*, June 8, 2015, https://ww w.theatlantic.com/politics/archive/2015/06/americas-largest-mental-hospital-is-a-jail/395012/.

23. RSA 2000, c M-13.

24. Wolff, "Fact Sheet: Incarceration and Mental Health."

25. Ibid.

26. G. Nelson, "Mental Health Policy in Canada," in *Canadian Social Policy: Issues and Perspectives*, by A. Westhues (Waterloo: Wilfrid Laurier University Press, 2006), 249.

27. See, e.g., Corinna Lain, "The Road to Hell Is Paved with Good Intentions: Deinstitutionalization and Mass Incarceration Nation," *William & Mary Law Review* 65 (2024), https://papers.ssr n.com/sol3/papers.cfm?abstract_id=4695644.

28. Wolff, "Fact Sheet: Incarceration and Mental Health."

29. Ibid.

30. Ibid.

31. Lain, "The Road to Hell is Paved with Good Intentions," 19-20.

32. Alison Read, "Psychiatric Deinstitutionalization in BC: Negative Consequences and Possible Solutions," *UBCMJ* 1, no. 1 (2009): 25.

33. So Steven Raphael and Michael A. Stoll, "Assessing the Contribution of the Deinstitutionaliza-tion of the Mentally Ill to Growth in the U.S. Incarceration Rate," *The Journal of Legal Studies* 42, no. 1 (2013): 187–222.

34. Alisa Roth, "The Truth about Deinstitutionalization," *The Atlantic*, May 25, 2021, https://w ww.theatlantic.com/health/archive/2021/05/truth-about-deinstitutionalization/618986/.

35. See, e.g., K.J. Aiello, "Who Gets to Be Mentally Ill?" *The Walrus*, December 2, 2022, https:/ /thewalrus.ca/who-gets-to-be-mentally-ill/; Esmé Weijun Wang, "Who Gets To Be The 'Good Schizophrenic'?," April 7, 2016, https://www.buzzfeednews.com/article/esmewwang/who-ge ts-to-be-the-good-schizophrenic.

36. Robert Goulden et al., "Newspaper Coverage of Mental Illness in the UK, 1992-2008," *BMC Public Health* 11:1 (2011), https://doi.org/10.1186/1471-2458-11-796 .

37. Shailee Koranne, "How Schizophrenia Is Misrepresented in TV and Film - and How We Can Do Better," *CBC*, March 29, 2022, https://www.cbc.ca/arts/how-schizophrenia-is-misrepresented -in-tv-and-film-and-how-we-can-do-better-1.6381980.

38. Aiello, "Who Gets to Be Mentally Ill?"

39. See Achille Mbembe, "Necropolitics," trans. Libby Meintjes, *Public Culture* 15, no. 1 (2003): 11–40.

40. Ibid, 40.

41. See "Preliminary Observations of the Operation of Correctional Service of Canada's Structured Intervention Units" (Public Safety Canada, October 26, 2021), https://www.publicsafety.gc.ca/cnt/rsrcs/pblctns/2022-siu-iap/index-en.aspx.

42. Ibid.

43. Ibid.

44. See Puar, *The Right to Maim*.

45. "Psychologist Testifies on the Risks of Solitary Confinement," *APA*, October 2012, Vol 43, No 9, https://www.apa.org/monitor/2012/10/solitary.

46. Stuart Grassian, "Psychiatric Effects of Solitary Confinement," *Washington University Journal of Law & Policy* 22 (2006): 325–83.

47. See Lauren Brinkley-Rubinstein et al., "Association of Restrictive Housing During Incarceration With Mortality After Release," *JAMA Netw Open* 2, no. 10 (2019), https://jamanetwork.com/journals/jamanetworkopen/fullarticle/2752350.

The Serpent's Bite

1. Ian A. McFarland, *In Adam's Fall: A Meditation on the Christian Doctrine of Original Sin*, Challenges in Contemporary Theology (Malden, MA: Wiley-Blackwell, 2010), 30.

2. Augustine, *Enchiridion: On Faith, Hope, and Love*, trans. Albert C. Outler, LCC (Louisville: Westminster John Knox, 1955), https://www.tertullian.org/fathers/augustine_enchiridion_02_trans.htm, sec 26.

3. Ibid, sec 45.

4. Ibid, sec 103.

5. McFarland, *In Adam's Fall*, 33 (emphasis original).

6. Augustine, *City of God*, trans. Marcus Dods (Peabody: Hendrickson, 2009), 16.8.

7. Augustine, *Enchiridion*, sec 91.

8. Ibid, sec 87.

9. Alison Kafer, *Feminist, Queer, Crip* (Bloomington: Indiana University Press, 2013), 28.

10. Ibid, 27.

11. Ibid, 28.

12. *Criminal Code*, RSC 1985, c C-46.

13. The clause was, historically, ibid, sec 745.6.

14. See, e.g., Tina Zhang & Lisa Ha, "An Analysis of the Use of the Faint Hope Clause" (Ottawa: Department of Justice Canada, 2010), https://www.canlii.org/en/commentary/doc/2010CanLI IDocs624#!fragment/zoupio-_Tocpdf_bk_1/, 1; Robin MacKay, "Legislative Summary of Bill S-6: An Act to Amend the Criminal Code and Another Act (Serious Time for the Most Serious Crime Act)" (Ottawa: Library of Parliament, 2010), https://lop.parl.ca/staticfiles/PublicWebs ite/Home/ResearchPublications/LegislativeSummaries/PDF/40-3/40-3-s6-e.pdf, sec 1.3.

15. Zhang & Ha, "An Analysis of the Use of the Faint Hope Clause," i.

16. "Tories to Repeal 'Faint Hope' Parole Clause," *CBC News*, June 5, 2009, https://www.cbc.ca/news/canada/tories-to-repeal-faint-hope-parole-clause-1.864611.

17. See the *Criminal Code*, sec 718.

18. So Marilyn McCord Adams, *Christ and Horrors: The Coherence of Christology*, Current Issues in Theology (Cambridge: Cambridge University Press, 2006), 36.

19. This is the thrust of my argument in Charlotte Dalwood, "Orthodoxy and the Politics of Christian Subjectivity: A Case Study of the Global Anglican Future Conference (GAFCON)," *Journal of Anglican Studies*, 2020, 1–13, https://doi.org/10.1017/S1740355320000145.

20. The Christian Church's genocidal campaign to eradicate the Indigenous peoples in what is now Canada is a case in point. On its theological dimensions, see, especially, Christina M. Conroy, "Theology After Residential Schools" (PhD diss., Atlanta, Emory University, 2016).

21. *R v Blackplume*, 2021 ABCA 2.

22. See *R v Blackplume*, 2019 ABPC 273.

23. See *Commissioner's Directive 100: Gender Diverse Offenders* (Ottawa: Correctional Service Canada, 2022), https://www.canada.ca/en/correctional-service/corporate/acts-regulations-pol icy/commissioners-directives/100.html, sec 36 and *passim*.

24. Ibid, sec 33 and *passim*.

25. See, e.g., Brooke Migdon, "LGBTQ+ rights groups defend California policy protecting transgender inmates," *The Hill*, May 10, 2022, https://thehill.com/changing-america/respect/equal ity/3483219-lgbtq-rights-groups-defend-california-policy-protecting-transgender-inmates/.

26. "Open Letter to The Canadian Association of Elizabeth Fry Societies," June 2, 2021, https://rapereliefshelter.bc.ca/wp-content/uploads/2021/06/updated-Letter-to-CAEFS-from-We-the-Criminalized-Women-PDF.pdf.

27. Ibid.

28. See, e.g., Alex Berg, "Analysis: How 'Toxic Masculinity' Fuels Transgender Victimization," *NBC News*, August 4, 2017, https://www.nbcnews.com/think/nbc-out/analysis-how-toxic-masculinity-fuels-transgender-victimization-ncna789621.

29. "Open Letter to The Canadian Association of Elizabeth Fry Societies."

30. See Charlotte Dalwood, "The De-Radicalization of an Anti-Trans Activist," *rabble.ca*, November 18, 2021, https://rabble.ca/lgbtiq/the-de-radicalization-of-an-anti-trans-activist/.

31. "The Issues," *CAWSBAR*, accessed May 14, 2024, https://www.cawsbar.ca/the-issues.

32. See, e.g., the documentation in Charlotte Dalwood, "As Misinformation Campaign against Transgender Rights Intensifies, Ottawa Must Act," *CBC News*, October 14, 2021, https://www.cbc.ca/news/opinion/opinion-transgender-rights-misinformation-campaign-charter-1.6207949.

33. So Lidia Abraha, "Defunding the Police Is Only the First Step to Abolition," *rabble.ca*, June 25, 2020, https://rabble.ca/general/defunding-police-only-first-step-abolitionism/.

34. See Statistics Canada, Government of Canada, "First Nations, Métis and Inuit Women," February 23, 2016, https://www150.statcan.gc.ca/n1/pub/89-503-x/2015001/article/14313-eng.htm.

35. See Corey Shefman, "Canada Must Reduce Soaring Number of Indigenous People in Jails," *National Observer*, May 18, 2022, https://www.nationalobserver.com/2022/05/18/opinion/canada-must-reduce-soaring-number-indigenous-people-jails.

36. "Crime Continues to Decline in Canada," *John Howard Society of Canada* (blog), April 30, 2022, https://johnhoward.ca/blog/crime-continues-to-decline-in-canada/.

37. Ivan Zinger, "Office of the Correctional Investigator Annual Report 2020-2021" (Ottawa: Office of the Correctional Investigator, June 30, 2021), https://oci-bec.gc.ca/en/content/office-correctional-investigator-annual-report-2020-2021.

38. Ibid.

39. Ibid.

40. See, e.g., "Quality of Life Policing," INCITE!, August 1, 2018, https://incite-national.org /quality-of-life-policing/; Eva Ureta and Jeff Shantz, "Here's Why We Can Abolish Most of the Criminal Justice System Now without Endangering Public Safety," *rabble.ca*, July 23, 2020, https://rabble.ca/politics/canadian-politics/heres-why-we-can-abolish-most-criminal-justice-system-now-without-endangering-public/.

41. Peter Wagner and Wendy Sawyer, "States of Incarceration: The Global Context 2018," Prison Policy Initiative, June 2021, https://www.prisonpolicy.org/global/2021.html.

42. David J. Harding, "Do Prisons Make Us Safer?," *Scientific American*, June 21, 2019, https://www.scientificamerican.com/article/do-prisons-make-us-safer/.

43. See, e.g., "Gender Violence & Race," INCITE!, July 31, 2018, https://incite-national.org/gender-violence-race/.

44. "Prison Abolition in Canada," *Upping the Anti* 4 (October 26, 2009), https://uppingtheanti.org/journal/article/04-prison-abolition-in-canada.

45. See the "Statement of Faith" (Christian and Missionary Alliance in Canada, 2018), https://www.cmacan.org/wp-content/uploads/2018/08/statement-of-faith.pdf.

46. See, further, the discussion of "slow death" in Lauren Berlant, *Cruel Optimism* (Durham, NC: Duke University Press, 2011).

47. Rosie DiManno, "Why Can't We Say 'Woman' Anymore?," *Toronto Star*, October 15, 2021, https://archive.ph/2021.10.19-140408/https://www.thestar.com/opinion/star-columnists/2021/10/15/why-cant-we-say-woman-anymore.html#selection-1397.29-1423.154.

48. Kathleen Stock, "Changing the Concept of 'Woman' Will Cause Unintended Harms," *The Economist*, July 6, 2018, https://www.economist.com/open-future/2018/07/06/changing-the-concept-of-woman-will-cause-unintended-harms.

49. Melissa Gira Grant, "'Grooming' Is Republicans' Cruel New Buzzword for Targeting Trans Kids," *The New Republic*, March 17, 2022, https://newrepublic.com/article/165761/republican-governors-grooming-crt-trans-rights.

50. See, e.g., Madeleine Carlisle, "Anti-Trans Violence and Rhetoric Reached Record Highs Across America in 2021," *Time*, December 30, 2021, https://time.com/6131444/2021-anti-trans-violence/ .

51. Janice G Raymond, *The Transsexual Empire: The Making of the She-Male* (Boston: Beacon Press, 1979).

52. "'Not All Transwomen,'" Women's Liberation Front, accessed May 27, 2024, https://womensliberationfront.org/encyclopedia-of-bad-gender-arguments/not-all-transwomen.

53. Ibid.

54. See "Sexual Assault: The Numbers | Responding to Transgender Victims of Sexual Assault," accessed May 27, 2024, https://ovc.ojp.gov/sites/g/files/xyckuh226/files/pubs/forge/sexual_n umbers.html.

55. "Transgender People over Four Times More Likely than Cisgender People to Be Victims of Violent Crime," Williams Institute, accessed May 27, 2024, https://williamsinstitute.law.ucla. edu/press/ncvs-trans-press-release/.

56. Jaime M. Grant, Lisa A. Mottet, and Justin Tanis, "Injustice at Every Turn: A Report of the National Transgender Discrimination Survey" (Washington: National Center for Transgender Equality and National Gay and Lesbian Task Force, 2011).

Paranoid Reading, Paranoia

1. Yale University is, of course, important as a setting in its own right for the history of critical literary theory. See, e.g., Marc Redfield, *Theory at Yale: The Strange Case of Deconstruction in America* (New York: Fordham University Press, 2015).

2. Eve Kosofsky Sedgwick, "Paranoid Reading and Reparative Reading, or, You're So Paranoid, You Probably Think This Essay Is About You," in *Touching Feeling: Affect, Pedagogy, Performativity*, Series Q (Durham, NC: Duke University Press, 2003), 123–51.

3. Paranoid reading is Sedgwick's psychoanalytically infused term for what Paul Ricoeur labels "the hermeneutics of suspicion" in Paul Ricoeur, *Freud and Philosophy: An Essay on Interpretation*, trans. Denis Savage (New Haven: Yale University Press, 1970), 33-35.

4. Sedgwick, "Paranoid Reading and Reparative Reading," 130.

5. Ibid, 129-130.

6. Ibid, 130.

7. Ibid, 131-133.

8. Ibid, 135-136.

9. Ibid, 136-138.

10. Ibid, 138-143.

11. It saturates the work of even those scholars who operate under the banner of "postcritique:" e.g., Rita Felski, *The Limits of Critique* (Chicago: University of Chicago Press, 2015).

12. See, e.g., Joel S. Baden, *The Composition of the Pentateuch: Renewing the Documentary Hypothesis*, The Anchor Yale Bible Reference Library (New Haven: Yale University Press, 2012).

13. The foundational work on social constructionism remains Peter L. Berger and Thomas Luckmann, *The Social Construction of Reality: A Treatise in the Sociology of Knowledge* (Garden City, NY: Doubleday, 1966).

14. On the ontological effect of cultural matrices, see, especially, Judith Butler, *Gender Trouble: Feminism and the Subversion of Identity* (London: Routledge, 1990), chap 1.

15. Quoted in Jacques Derrida, "Structure, Sign and Play in the Discourse of the Human Sciences," in *Writing and Difference*, trans. Alan Bass (London: Routledge, 2006), 351.

16. See, e.g., Aninda B. Acharya and Juan Carlos Sánchez-Manso, "Anosognosia," in *StatPearls* (Treasure Island: StatPearls Publishing, 2024), http://www.ncbi.nlm.nih.gov/books/NBK513361/.

17. Sedgwick, "Paranoid Reading and Reparative Reading," 138.

18. So "Most Popular Car Colors in America," Edmunds, accessed May 18, 2024, https://www.edmunds.com/most-popular-car-colors/.

19. See, e.g., Phyllis Trible, *Texts of Terror: Literary-Feminist Readings of Biblical Narratives*, Overtures to Biblical Theology (Philadelphia: Fortress, 1984).

Being Damned, Being Trans

1. Adapted from Berlie Custis, trans., "The Life of Adam and Eve," accessed May 17, 2024, https://www2.iath.virginia.edu/anderson/vita/english/vita.lat.html.

2. The original, and still definitive, theorization of transmisogyny is Julia Serano, *Whipping Girl: A Transsexual Woman on Sexism and the Scapegoating of Femininity*, 2nd ed. (New York: Seal Press, 2016).

3. See, e.g., "Gender-Based Violence against Trans Women Claims More Lives," *National Center for Transgender Equality* (blog), August 12, 2015, https://transequality.org/blog/gender-based-violence-against-trans-women-claims-more-lives; "Fatal Violence against the Transgender and Gender-Expansive Community in 2020," Human Rights Campaign, accessed May 17, 2024, https://www.hrc.org/resources/violence-against-the-trans-and-gender-expansive-community-in-2020; "Fighting Anti-Trans Violence," Lambda Legal, accessed May 17, 2024, https://legacy.lambdalegal.org/know-your-rights/article/trans-violence.

4. See, e.g., "Transgender People and Suicide," Centre for Suicide Prevention, May 6, 2019, https://www.suicideinfo.ca/local_resource/trans-fact-sheet/.

5. "Members of the Episcopal Church," Religious Landscape Study (Pew Research Center), accessed May 17, 2024, https://www.pewresearch.org/religious-landscape-study/database/religious-denomination/episcopal-church/.

6. See The Office of the General Convention, ed., *Constitution and Canons Together with The Rules of Order* (New York: The Domestic and Foreign Missionary Society of The Episcopal Church, 2018), Canon I.17.5.

7. See Laurie Goodstein, "Openly Gay Man Is Made a Bishop," *New York Times*, November 3, 2003, https://www.nytimes.com/2003/11/03/us/openly-gay-man-is-made-a-bishop.html.

8. Stephen Bates, "Gene Robinson's Losing Battle to Be Known as Simply 'The Bishop,'" *The Guardian*, November 7, 2010, https://www.theguardian.com/world/2010/nov/07/gene-robinson-losing-battle-bishop.

9. Jude Sheerin, "Matthew Shepard: The Murder That Changed America," *BBC*, October 26, 2018, https://www.bbc.com/news/world-us-canada-45968606.

10. See *The Book of Occasional Services: Conforming to General Convention 2018*, 2018, 120-124.

11. See, e.g., "'A Service of Renaming' Approved for Use Across the Episcopal Church," *Trans Episcopal* (blog), July 23, 2018, https://www.transepiscopal.org/blog/a-renaming-service-for-the-episcopal-church.

12. The decline of The Episcopal Church is well documented. See, e.g., Egan Millard, "2019 Parochial Reports Show Continued Decline and a 'Dire' Future for The Episcopal Church," *Episcopal News Service*, October 16, 2020, https://episcopalnewsservice.org/2020/10/16/2019-parochial-reports-show-continued-decline-and-a-dire-future-for-the-episcopal-church/.

13. The Episcopal Church largely uses the NRSV translation in its public worship, and, in this chapter, so do I.

14. Robert W. Jenson, "Evil as Person," in *Theology as Revisionary Metaphysics: Essays on God and Creation*, ed. Stephen John Wright (Eugene, OR: Wipf & Stock, 2014), 136–45.

15. Ibid, 140.

16. Ibid.

17. Ibid.

18. Jules Gill-Peterson, "Paranoia as a Trans Style: The Situation Comedy of Trans Life," Substack, *Sad Brown Girl* (blog), February 2, 2021, https://sadbrowngirl.substack.com/p/paranoia-as-a-trans-style.

19. Jules Gill-Peterson, "'Just a Bunch of Hot F*ck Ups': The Trans Comedy of Dissociation and Wanting to Be Normal," Substack, *Sad Brown Girl* (blog), February 9, 2021, https://sadbrowngirl.substack.com/p/just-a-bunch-of-hot-fck-ups.

20. Catholic Church, *Catechism of the Catholic Church: Revised in Accordance with the Official Latin Text Promulgated by Pope John Paul II* (Washington, DC: United States Catholic Conference, 2000).

21. See, e.g., Alexandra Holden, "The Gay/Trans Panic Defense: What It Is, and How to End It," *ABA*, Summer 2019, https://www.americanbar.org/groups/crsj/publications/member-features/gay-trans-panic-defense/.

22. "Journal of the 77th General Convention of the Protestant Episcopal Church in the United States of America Otherwise Known as The Episcopal Church 2012" (The Archives of the Episcopal Church, 2022), https://www.episcopalarchives.org/sites/default/files/publications/2012_GC_Journal.pdf.

23. "The 2022 Episcopal Clergy Compensation Report" (Church Pension Group, December 2023), https://www.cpg.org/globalassets/documents/publications/report-2022-clergy-compensation-report.pdf.

24. *Remarks by The Right Rev. V. Gene Robinson* (Washington National Cathedral, 2021), https://www.youtube.com/watch?v=Y7V3QH43LUM.

25. David Paulsen, "National Cathedral Criticized for Inviting Max Lucado to Preach Despite Pastor's Anti-LGBTQ Views," *Episcopal News Service*, February 5, 2021, https://episcopalnewsservice.org/2021/02/05/national-cathedral-criticized-for-inviting-max-lucado-to-preach-despite-pastors-anti-lgbtq-views/.

26. C.S. Lewis, *The Great Divorce*, Revised Edition (New York: HarperOne, 2015).

PART FIVE

1. Marin Sardy, *The Edge of Every Day: Sketches of Schizophrenia* (New York: Vintage, 2020).

2. I learned later that the research confirms my intuition. Cognitive deficits, including memory problems, are now recognized as a core feature of schizophrenia. See, e.g., Christopher R. Bowie and Philip D. Harvey, "Cognitive Deficits and Functional Outcome in Schizophrenia," *Neuropsychiatry Dis Treat.* 2, no. 4 (2006): 531–36.

A Future for Eve

1. Joshua Schreier, trans., *Bereshit Rabbah* (Sefaria, 2022), https://www.sefaria.org/Bereshit_Rabbah.20.11?lang=bi, 20.11.

2. *Exorcisms and Related Supplications: English Translation According to the Typical Edition* (Washington, D.C.: International Commission on English in the Liturgy Corporation, 2017).

3. "Exorcism: Vatican Course Opens Doors to 250 Priests," *BBC*, April 16, 2018, https://www.bbc.com/news/world-europe-43697573.

4. *The Book of Common Prayer, and Administration of the Sacraments, and Other Rites, and Ceremonies of the Church, Together with The Psalter or Psalms of David: According to the Use of The Episcopal Church* (New York: Church Publishing, 1979), 302.

5. *The Book of Occasional Services: Conforming to General Convention 2018*, 2018, 195.

6. *The Book of Occasional Services*, 167.

7. Paul Ricoeur, *The Symbolism of Evil*, trans. Emerson Buchanan (Boston: Beacon, 1967).

8. Ibid, 351.

9. Ibid, 350-351.

10. Ibid, 352.

11. Ibid, 350.

12. One of the best overviews of what all is involved, on a personal as well as a communal level, is Anita Diamant, *Choosing a Jewish Life: A Handbook for People Converting to Judaism and for Their Family and Friends* (New York: Schocken, 1998).

13. William Davidson, trans., "Tractate Sanhedrin," in *Koren Talmud Bavli*, vol. 1, 2017, 37a.

14. The foregoing is the overarching argument in Jeffrey A. Lieberman, *Malady of the Mind: Schizophrenia and the Path to Prevention* (New York: Scribner, 2023).

15. Elyse D. Frishman, ed., *Mishkan T'filah: A Reform Siddur* (New York: CCAR Press, 2007), 251

A Past for Adam

1. "Nashville Statement: A Coalition for Biblical Sexuality" (Council for Biblical Manhood and Womanhood, August 29, 2017), under "Preamble," https://cbmw.org/nashville-statement/.

2. Ibid, Articles 1-2, 9.

3. Ibid, Article 10.

4. See, e.g., "A Liturgists Statement," The Liturgists, August 29, 2017, http://www.theliturgists .com/statement; Antonia Blumberg, "Evangelical Leaders Release Anti-LGBTQ Statement on Human Sexuality," *Huffington Post*, August 29, 2017, https://www.huffingtonpost.com/entry/ evangelical-leaders-nashville-statement_us_59a5b705e4b00795c2a217fc; Brian McLaren, "Why I Applaud (and Fervently Deny) the Nashville Statement," Auburn Seminary, accessed April 30, 2018, http://auburnseminary.org/applaud-fervently-deny-nashville-statement/.

5. See the preamble in "Christians United In Support of LGBT+ Inclusion in the Church: The Statement," Christians United, August 30, 2017, http://www.christiansunitedstatement.org.

6. See, e.g., J.I. Packer, *Rediscovering Holiness: Know the Fullness of Life with God*, 2nd ed. (Grand Rapids: Baker, 2009), 139; J.I. Packer, *Engaging the Written Word of God* (Peabody, MA: Hendrickson, 2012), 126.

7. Justin Taylor, "The Five Authors Who Have Most Influenced J.I. Packer," *The Gospel Coalition*, May 14, 2013, https://www.thegospelcoalition.org/blogs/justin-taylor/the-five-authors-who -have-most-influenced-j-i-packer/. For the purposes of this chapter, references to the *Institutes* are to John Calvin, *Institutes of the Christian Religion*, ed. John T. McNeill, trans. Ford Lewis Battles, 2 vols., LCC 20–21 (Louisville: Westminster John Knox, 1960).

8. A point exploited for humorous effect in a 1983 "interview" with the reformer printed in *Vanity Fair*. For a discussion of this parody and its implications for understanding the power of the *Institutes* to "continue to draw new readers," see Bruce Gordon, *John Calvin's Institutes of the Christian Religion*, Lives of Great Religious Books (Princeton: Princeton University Press, 2016), 8–12.

9. See Roland Boer, "Night Sprinkle(s): Pornography and the Song of Songs," in *Knockin' On Heaven's Door: The Bible and Popular Culture*, Biblical Limits (London: Routledge, 1999), 53–70.

10. In employing the notion of domains of intelligibility, I am informed by the discussion of frames, recognition, and intelligibility in Judith Butler, *Precarious Life: The Powers of Mourning and Violence* (London: Verso, 2004); Judith Butler, *Frames of War: When Is Life Grievable?*, Radical Thinkers (London: Verso, 2016).

11. See Jacques Derrida, *Specters of Marx: The State of the Debt, the Work of Mourning and the New International*, trans. Peggy Kamuf (New York: Routledge, 1994), 18–25; Jacques Derrida and Elisabeth Roudinesco, *For What Tomorrow...: A Dialogue*, trans. Jeff Fort, Cultural Memory in the Present (Stanford: Stanford University Press, 2004), 3–8.

12. Derrida and Roudinesco, *For What Tomorrow*, 5.

13. The language of fanaticism is borrowed from Tillich, *The Courage To Be*. See, further, the related discussion of authoritarianism apropos of dogma in David Tracy, *The Analogical Imagination: Christian Theology and the Culture of Pluralism* (New York: Crossroad, 1981), 99.

14. In this sense, they are what Sedgwick terms "fantasy books," namely, those that "have a presence, or exert a pressure in our lives and thinking, that may have much or little to do with what's actually inside them" (Eve Kosofsky Sedgwick, "Melanie Klein and the Difference Affect Makes," *South Atlantic Quarterly* 106, no. 3 (2007): 625).

15. For a discussion of this example in relation to contemporary trends in the interpretation and appropriation of the *Institutes*, see Gordon, *Calvin's Institutes*, chap. 12 (esp. pp. 208-10). Note that at the time of the article's publication (November), Keller had not yet completed his reading of Calvin's text.

16. Timothy Keller, "The Counterintuitive Calvin," *The Gospel Coalition*, November 12, 2012, https://www.thegospelcoalition.org/reviews/the-counterintuitive-calvin/.

17. Timothy Keller, "Christianity and Homosexuality: A Review of Books," October 4, 2013, http://www.timothykeller.com/blog/2013/10/4/christianity-and-homosexuality-a-review-of-books.

18. Ibid (emphasis original); cf. Timothy Keller and Kathy Keller, *The Meaning of Marriage: Facing the Complexities of Commitment with the Wisdom of God* (New York: Riverhead, 2011), e.g., 205, 284.

19. Gordon, *Calvin's Institutes*, 217.

20. *Inst.* I.v.1,10.

21. *Inst.* I.ii.2. See, further, Randall C. Zachman, *The Assurance of Faith: Conscience in the Theology of Martin Luther and John Calvin* (Minneapolis: Fortress, 1993), 104.

22. *Inst.* I.ii.1.

23. *Inst.* I.v.3.

24. *Inst.* I.ii.1-2; I.v.3,9. See, further, Zachman, *The Assurance of Faith*, 104–5.

25. *Inst.* I.ii.1.

26. See, e.g., *Inst.* I.v.9.

27. *Inst.* I.ii.2. See Zachman, *The Assurance of Faith*, 106.

28. Serene Jones, *Calvin and the Rhetoric of Piety*, Columbia Series in Reformed Theology (Louisville: Westminster John Knox, 1995), 132.

29. *Inst.* I.ii.1, emphasis mine. See further Jones, *Calvin and the Rhetoric of Piety*, chap. 4

30. It is the confusion of the finite with Divinity that Tillich rightly terms the demonic; see Tillich, *Systematic Theology* 1:140, and *passim*.

31. See further the discussion of the secular in Tillich, *Systematic Theology* 1:218.

32. *Inst.* I.ii.2.

33. Sedgwick, "Paranoid Reading, Reparative Reading," 149. In *Sex, or the Unbearable*, 41–46, Lee Edelman critiques Sedgwick's account of reparative reading for remaining within the very "dualistic thinking she associates with paranoia." Correctly, he notes that "the reparative aesthetic emerges by breaking from the breaking characteristic of paranoia," and that it thereby reduplicates the structure of paranoia itself. While that reduplication implies that the reparative is, by virtue of being so, also a paranoiac (although not that the paranoiac is a reparative), it does so because it indicates that the reparative reader is inheriting a paranoid critical tradition. Sedgwick acknowledges as much when she recognizes "the centrality" of both D.A. Miller's *The Novel and the Police* and Judith Butler's *Gender Trouble* (her two principal examples of paranoid reading practices in "Paranoid Reading, Reparative Reading") "to the development of my own thought, and that of the critical movements that most interest me" ("Paranoid Reading, Reparative Reading," 129). Sedgwick's delineation of reparativity is, in other words, indebted to the marquee statements of the very critical practices it challenges; more, as Edelman astutely discerns, it advances the same stream of methodologically suspicious interpretive theory to which it objects. All of which is to say that it exemplifies the sort of creative, but recognizably continuous, engagement with the tradition that elected it that, I have argued here, the inheritor performs, with Sedgwick *qua* heir assuming responsibility for a paranoid theoretical archive the contents of which she thereby undertakes to repair. That "reparativity repeats the schizoid practice it claims to depart from" (Berlant and Edeman, *Sex, or the Unbearable*, 44) is thus not so much its undoing as that which allows the reparative to speak so powerfully to critics in the contemporary theoretical moment.

34. Sedgwick, "Paranoid Reading, Reparative Reading," 146.

35. Derrida and Roudinesco, *For What Tomorrow*, 4.

36. In thinking through the possibilities for coalition building between progressive and conservative groups and discourses, I find a productive conversation partner in Andrea Smith, *Native Americans and the Christian Right: The Gendered Politics of Unlikely Alliances* (Durham, NC: Duke University Press, 2008).

37. "Nashville Statement," under "Preamble."

Until At Dawn We Wake

1. Gail Murphy-Geiss, "Report on Gender-Based and Sexual Misconduct in The Episcopal Church for The Task Force for Women, Truth and Reconciliation," in *Reports to the 80th General Convention*, vol. 3 (New York: The Domestic and Foreign Missionary Society of the Protestant Episcopal Church in the United States of America, 2021), 969–92.

2. Dawn Wiggins Hare et al., "Sexual Misconduct in The United Methodist Church: US Update" (Resource UMC, n.d.), https://www.resourceumc.org/en/partners/gcsrw/home/content/sexual-misconduct-in-the-united-methodist-church-us-update-general-commission-on-the-status-and-role.

3. "LGBTQ+ in the Church" (The Episcopal Church, n.d.), https://www.episcopalchurch.org/organizations-affiliations/lgbtq/.

4. See David Paulsen, "Fallout from Washington National Cathedral Guest Preacher a 'Teachable Moment' for the Church," *Episcopal News Service*, February 9, 2021, https://www.episcopalnewsservice.org/2021/02/09/fallout-from-washington-national-cathedral-guest-preacher-a-teachable-moment-for-the-church/.

5. *Remarks by The Right Rev. V. Gene Robinson* (Washington National Cathedral, 2021), https://www.youtube.com/watch?v=Y7V3QH43LUM.

6. Chico Harlan and Sarah Pulliam Bailey, "Pope Francis Says Priests Cannot Bless Same-Sex Unions, Dashing Hopes of Gay Catholics," *Washington Post*, March 16, 2021, https://www.washingtonpost.com/world/europe/pope-same-sex-unions-licit/2021/03/15/8c51ee80-8581-11eb-be4a-24b89f616f2c_story.html.

7. See, e.g., Egan Millard, "Former Albany Bishop William Love Leaves The Episcopal Church to Join ACNA," *Episcopal News Service*, March 30, 2021, https://www.episcopalnewsservice.org/2021/03/30/former-albany-bishop-william-love-leaves-the-episcopal-church-to-join-acna/.

8. The preceding portion of this chapter first appeared, in an earlier version, on Religion Dispatches (http://www.religiondispatches.org), which is a publication of Political Research Associates (http://www.politicalresearch.org).

To contact Charlotte Dalwood for speaking engagements,
please visit www.charlottedalwood.com.

Many Voices. One Message.

quoir.com